Literature for Youth

Series Editor: Edward T. Sullivan

The World of Islam in Literature for Youth

A Selective Annotated Bibliography for K–12

Rajinder Garcha
Patricia Yates Russell

Literature for Youth, No. 7

The Scarecrow Press, Inc.
Lanham, Maryland • Toronto • Oxford
2006

SCARECROW PRESS, INC.

Published in the United States of America
by Scarecrow Press, Inc.
A wholly owned subsidary of
The Rowman & Littlefield Publishing Group, Inc.
4501 Forbes Boulevard, Suite 200, Lanham, Maryland 20706
www.scarecrowpress.com

PO Box 317
Oxford
OX2 9RU, UK

British Library Cataloguing in Publication Information Available

Library of Congress Cataloging-in-Publication Data

Garcha, Rajinder.
  The world of Islam in literature for youth : a selective annotated biblio-
graphy for k-12 / Rajinder Garcha, Patricia Yates Russell.
    p. cm. — (Literature for youth ; 7)
  Includes bibliographical references and index.
  ISBN-13: 978-0-8108-5488-8 (pbk. : alk. paper)
  ISBN-10: 0-8108-5488-0 (pbk. : alk. paper)
  1. Islam—Juvenile literature—Bibliography.   I. Russell, Patricia Yates,
1937-   . II. Title. III. Series.
  Z7835.M6G27 2006
  [BP161.3]
  016.297—dc22
                                                              2005026645

∞™ The paper used in this publication meets the minimum requirements of
American National Standard for Information Sciences—Permanence of Paper
for Printed Library Materials, ANSI/NISO Z39.48-1992.
Manufactured in the United States of America.

This book is dedicated to our late mothers,
Mrs. Tej Sidhu and Mrs. Carrie Jatho Yates respectively,
for the inspiration they have given us.

Contents

Foreword

In the twenty-first century (AD), Islam represents a numerically large and socially influential component of Western societies. Yet many Westerners are woefully uninformed about the nature, history, and potentialities that this religion and its civilization have contributed to the past, are contributing to the present, and can contribute to the future of human civilization. Many resources for learning about Islam are available, but most are not prominently featured in existing bibliographies, databases, and libraries. A number of the most useful and available resources have been carefully selected and insightfully reviewed by Ms. Garcha and Ms. Russell. Their work is motivated by a desire to make reliable information available about this often-misunderstood religious tradition and its civilizational influence.

Islam arose in western Arabia in the early seventh century (AD) within a context influenced by Judaism, Christianity, and ancient, non-specific biblical roots. It recognizes the authority of the Hebrew Bible and of the Christian New Testament but considers these supplemented and, in part, superseded by its own, the Qur'an—a revelation received by the prophet Muhammad. It also recognizes the authority of the biblical prophets such as Abraham, Moses, David, and Jesus—whom Islam venerates as a great prophet but NOT as a divine figure. Islamic belief is radically monotheistic and its important practices include prayer, fasting, almsgiving, and pilgrimage. It thus shares much with Judaism and Christianity but is little known and perhaps less understood by most Jews and most Christians. This ignorance is unfortunate and indeed puzzling given Islam's prominence on the stage of world events.

Islam is, after all, the second largest and the fastest growing religion in the world. It is almost daily acquiring a heightened profile in the public awareness of Western countries, including prominently the United States of America. Some estimates place the Muslim population of the United States at six million, making it a rival with Judaism for first place among non-Christian religions in the country. This figure is perhaps somewhat inflated; but even the most conservative of estimates place the number at two to three million—larger than most individual Protestant denominations. By any measure, Islam has become a significant presence in and a prominent influence upon most Western societies; and this influence is actually not anything new.

For almost a millennium (roughly the 600s to the 1600s AD), Islamic civilizations in southern and western Asia and in northern Africa were probably among the most advanced and prosperous on earth. Certainly, for a large portion of that time, the Islamic societies on the southern and eastern rim of the Mediterranean dwarfed their Christian rivals to the north and west in literary, philosophical, scientific, and mathematical learning as well as in material prosperity and in military might. The philosophical heritage of the Greeks, the mathematical heritage of the Indians, the alchemical heritage of the Egyptians, and the astronomical heritage of the Arabs were all mediated to Christian Europe by their Muslim Arab neighbors on the south shore of the mid-land sea. Economically and politically strong, intellectually and culturally confident, Muslim societies were places of enlightened thought in literature, philosophy, mathematics, science, etc. Meanwhile, in Christian lands, the scientists, the philosophers, and the literati huddled in the benighted corners of the Dark Ages.

Circumnavigation of Africa and then of the globe in the sixteenth-century era dealt a severe blow to the economic dominance of Muslim civilization by opening direct trade between Christian Europe and non-Muslim south and east Asia. Concomitantly, the vast resources of the Americas enriched and emboldened Europeans in their competition and rivalry with their southern neighbors. As economic and political superiority passed from Muslim into Christian hands, so too did the competence to claim for themselves the right to be heirs of the intellectual and cultural heritage of much of humankind. Likewise passed the confidence to proclaim themselves the chosen innovators and the authoritative definers of the future of human discoveries. Meanwhile, the Muslim world, outflanked economically, weakened militarily, and overshadowed intellectually, fell into its own sort of Dim Ages.

It is only in the past five centuries or so that the Christian-influenced culture of Europe and the Americas could come to think of itself as the dominant and, in many cases, as the only culture of global significance. Western economic and political hegemony led to the West's view of itself as the finest expression of cultural, intellectual, and technological development in the course of human history. And finest it may have been, but the concomitant conceit was that Western culture was not only the finest but also the final expression of human development. The idea that other cultures, other religions, other areas of the world might rise to prominence in civilization's evolution was basically inconceivable. Similarly, residents of the West, particularly of the United States, somehow managed to remain oblivious as a rising tide of non-Christian, non-European, non-Western immigrants moved into their country, their cities, their neighborhoods, their blocks and culs-de-sac. After five hundred years of defining the world in its own terms, the West found itself living elbow-to-elbow with that world and itself being defined by the neighbors—particularly, the Muslim neighbors.

Geo-politically this new reality meant that once again the Muslim world must be reckoned into the calculations and decisions of Western political and economic planners. From the oil reserves of the Persian Gulf to the tropical forest harvests of Indonesia and Malaysia and from the reinvestment of petrodollars in Western economies by wealthy Arabian sheiks to the outsourcing of low-paying manufacturing jobs to Pakistani child laborers, the West again finds that the Muslim civilization it once disdained is now the very civilization with which it must reckon.

Locally a religion and a people which once seemed too exotic to imagine except in fables and fantasies are now a part of the neighborhood. From questions of the tax-exempt status of Muslim religious properties to provisions for the serving of *halal* meats in cafeterias and from providing "chaplaincy" services to Muslims in the military to allowing time and place for mid-day prayer by Muslim students in public schools, many Western community leaders find that the very Muslims they once ignored are now the citizens whose votes they must court for election, levy funds, etc.

Yet those who desire to know more about Islam and to understand its place in our world and in our time are often bewildered as to where to start. Historians may point them to some authoritative multi-volume history of Muslim civilization; literati may point them to the beautiful but mystifying metaphors of Islamic poetry; social scientists may trot out the most recent analysis of the middle-eastern quagmire; and pious Muslims may point them to the powerful but sometimes opaque Qur'anic scripture. But none of these is likely to be the best place to start learning or, more importantly, teaching about a religious and cultural tradition of such complexity.

Ms. Garcha and Ms. Russell provide teachers as well as preachers, librarians as well as laypersons, with useful guidance on where to begin learning and how to begin teaching about Islam. This bibliography is selective rather than exhaustive, but it is wisely selective of available print and other resources classified by topic and annotated as to appropriate age level. Whether selecting for one's own learning, for effective teaching, or for collection development, it should be of great assistance in overcoming our woeful ignorance of those with whom we share the planet, the nation, and perhaps the block.

R. Blake Michael, Ph.D.
Swan-Collins-Allen Professor of
    World Religion and Christian Missions
Ohio Wesleyan University
Delaware, Ohio

Dr. R. Blake Michael is Swan-Collins-Allen Professor of World Religions and Christian Missions at Ohio Wesleyan University in Delaware, Ohio, where he is Associate Dean of Academic Affairs. He has also served as Visiting Professor of World Religions at the Methodist Theological School in Ohio.

Acknowledgments

While preparing this annotated bibliography, the authors have become indebted to a number of individuals whose gracious assistance and support have made it possible for its completion. We are thankful to Mrs. Manal M. El-Sheikh and Ms. Nabeela Hamdan, teachers at the Islamic Center of Greater Toledo, for their guidance and advice in selection of some of the resources from the Islamic Center for this book. The authors were always made welcome and comfortable during their visits to the center to research materials available there.

Dr. Lois Buttlar, a professor of library and information science at Kent State University and a well-known researcher in her field, provided invaluable constructive suggestions that helped the authors in improving the organization of this book.

The authors are especially grateful to Mr. Mark Horan, a librarian at the University of Toledo, for his unstinting encouragement and his creative solutions to calls for technical help. His insight and knowledge as a librarian opened doors for us, and his facility with creating databases helped us tremendously. Finally, his invaluable time in creating all the indexes for this book is greatly appreciated.

We thank the staff of Harrow Public Library in the United Kingdom, the members of the OhioLINK libraries, as well as the Toledo-Lucas County Public Library, for providing resources for this book. Thanks are also due to the University of Toledo Committee on Sabbaticals for granting one of the authors, Ms. Garcha, sabbatical leave for one semester to allow her to work on this project. In addition, we are very grateful to the Islamic Center of Greater Toledo for allowing us to use the photograph of the lovely Center for the cover of our book.

Finally, thanks to our families and friends for their understanding that the time the project took us from them was necessary in order to meet the deadline for the completion of this book.

Every attempt has been made by the authors to ensure accuracy and consistency regarding information contained in this book. However, the authors apologize for any inaccuracies, omissions, or any inconsistency herein. Any slights of people, places, or organizations are unintentional. The discretion of teachers, parents, and librarians should be used to consider carefully the resources that they need to use for educational purposes.

Introduction

For many years non-Muslims and Muslims have lived together without feeling the need to understand each other in terms of religion and culture. There was not much interest among people to learn about the Muslims, the second largest religion in the world. The Black Muslim movement in the 1930s in the United States was America's main exposure to Islam. Today, due to political, economic, and other reasons, this is not the case any longer. The modern world is interwoven and interlinked. There are millions of Muslims who live in Western countries, and there are thousands of individuals from the West working in some of the Muslim countries. Although there may be a genuine willingness for both the Westerners and the Muslims to learn about each other's culture and religion, it seems that both groups have problems—perhaps due to past hostile experiences dating back to the eras of the rise of Islamic expansionism and the Christian crusades.

The September 11, 2001, tragic destruction of the World Trade Center towers in New York City, the Pentagon, and other terrorist attacks worldwide have captured the attention of both scholars and lay people. Countries like Afghanistan and Iraq, previously given little attention in the social studies content for American schoolchildren, have now become part of everyday television news coverage along with mention of Holy War, Jihad, Allah, and women hidden behind mysterious veils. How do educators and parents explain these images as part of the school curriculum? How can they identify instructional materials that provide information related to the Muslim culture and, in particular, the religion of Islam? Earlier guides such as *Building Ethnic Collections: An Annotated Guide for School Media Centers and Public Libraries* have not been updated; their attention to Muslims in the Middle East and other countries is extremely limited.[1] This reference book should help to provide an international understanding and enlighten the reading public, including Muslim and non-Muslim children and adults alike; and therefore, be well informed of the Muslim culture and the religion of Islam.

Misconceptions, prejudices, and stereotypes exist due to the lack of understanding and ignorance regarding the religion of Islam. For example, the attack on the World Trade Center and the Pentagon on September 11th has been labeled by the press as an "Islamic terrorist" attack. Also, many Muslims, in the "eyes," or perceptions of some Westerners, carry the burden of guilt for the September 11th tragedy. Ignorance breeds prejudice. It is only through understanding and education that violence against people of a certain religion or faith can be eliminated. Educators and parents need to start teaching and educating children from a very young age so that they can grow into adults who are tolerant of cultural and religious differences. Since Islam is one of the fastest growing religions in the world, it is in the interest of non-Muslims to gain an understanding of this culture and religion.

According to the Central Intelligence Agency fact book (CIA), the most current information is that among every four humans in the world, one of them is a Muslim. Muslims have increased by over 235% in the last 50 years up to nearly 1.6 billion. The Muslim population of the major English speaking countries is as follows: Australia 382,000 (2.09%), Canada 400,000 (1.48%), the United Kingdom 1,579,229 (2.7%), and the United States 9,992,860 (3.75%). Currently, the total world population of Muslims is 1.6 billion. Most people believe that the majority of the followers of Islam are Arabs, but according to the data, there are more Muslims in non-Arab countries, such as Indonesia.[2]

METHODOLOGY

Identification of the resources selected for inclusion in this reference book was based on a comprehensive literature survey. Materials were evaluated based on the following criteria: positive reviews in standard selection tools

---

1. Buttlar, Lois, and Lubomyr Roman Wynar, *Building Ethnic Collections: An Annotated Guide for School Media Centers and Public Libraries* (Littleton, CO; 1977).

2. *The World Factbook*. 2005. The Central Intelligence Agency of the United States. January 7, 2005, <http://www.cia.gov/cia/publications/factbook/geos/ke.html>

such as *Booklist, Choice, School Library Journal,* and *Publisher's Weekly*; and the availability of the materials. Materials still in print were given preference, but when materials were limited for a particular subject or grade level, consideration was given to out-of-print titles that could be borrowed from other libraries and information centers since the literature for a particular subject is limited. For example, some of the resources were obtained for review from the Islamic Center of Greater Toledo. The knowledge of existence of these materials is important for teachers, students, parents, and librarians.

Titles for books and non-book materials were identified through *World-Cat; Films for the Humanities and Sciences, Bowker's Complete Video Directory, Video Source Book, OhioLINK (the consortium of libraries in Ohio), Books-in-Print online, Subject Guide to Books in Print,* and *Islamic websites.* Materials were chosen selectively based on the availability of the resources and quality of reviews appearing in selection tools for school, public, and academic library materials. Balancing the entries with respect to the grade level was taken into account. Due to the lack of materials or resources in some subject areas relevant to grade level, there was a disparity of entries. The majority of the annotations provided in this book are based on visual examination.

Scope and Arrangement of Material

This publication is aimed primarily at librarians, parents, students, teachers and school media specialists who are interested in identifying helpful resources on the topic of Islam and the Muslim culture. At the time of this writing, a literature review did not provide any evidence of existence of a similar reference guide in English.

This publication is divided into 16 chapters that reflect the different aspects of Islam and the Muslim culture for the K–12 level.

Complete entries provide information in the following sequence:

Art and Architecture
Biographies
    Muhammad
    Others
Curricular Resources
Digital Electronic Resources (encompasses various chapters which are included in print format)
Fiction and Folklore
General Reference Resources
Geography
History and Politics
Interreligious Studies
Islamic Faith and Practice
    Hadith
    Holy Days
    Muslim Culture and Customs
    Qur'an

Major Contributions
Muslims in the West
Nation of Islam
Resistance versus Terrorism
Women in Islam
Internet Resources (The list of websites has been organized alphabetically according to the majority of the above chapters as well.)

ENTRIES

Annotated entries provide a complete bibliographical description, including author's name, title, place of publication, publisher, year, paging, and ISBN (both for hard copy and paper, if available). The grade levels for each entry are indicated as best suited (e.g., K–4, 9–12).

Digital Electronic Resources, in addition to the above bibliographic description, also include length of running time, producer, black-and-white or color.

Internet Resources are included for supplemental information and may be used at one's discretion.

INDICES

The indices are comprised of an author index, geographic index, grade index, illustrator and photographer index, subject index, and title index.

1

Art and Architecture

In this chapter, one will find twelve resources pertaining to Islamic art and architecture — eight for high school, two for middle school, and two for elementary school grade levels. The period covers from the seventh century A.D. to the present time. It represents the Egyptian, Ottoman, Spanish, Moroccan, Persian, and South Asian areas.

1 *Splendors of Islam: Architecture, Decoration, and Design*
Clevenot, Dominique; photographs by Gerard Degeorge.
New York: Vendome Press, 2000. 224 pp.
ISBN: 2080135104
Grades 11–12
   The author covers four approaches to Islamic architectural ornamentation: an overview of Islamic architecture and its diversity, the techniques and the materials used by the builders and Muslim artists, Islamic ornamentation, and aesthetics. Each section has a "documentary notebook" containing photographs to allow a more complete examination of the topic. Brilliant colors complement the text. The book is translated from the French. "This truly beautiful book should be in both public and academic libraries." — *Library Journal*

2 *The Mosque: History, Architectural Development and Regional Diversity*
Frishman, Martin and Hasan-Uddin Khan, editors.
London: Thames & Hudson, 2002. 288 pp.
ISBN: 0500283451
Grade 12

More appropriate for students interested in art and architecture, this volume containing 378 illustrations, 170 in color, provides a wealth of information regarding the architecture of a mosque. In addition to serving as an excellent guide to an understanding of the role of mosques in Islamic society and culture around the world, this wonderful book provides the history and development of the mosque since it was originated in Medina and Mecca during the time of the Prophet Muhammad. Its traditional religious and teaching role among the Muslims, and its architectural and decorative features such as the mihrab, the dome, the minaret, are explained. It also discusses calligraphic inspirations and the use of geometric patterns which are widespread but vary in style. One of the chapters explores contemporary mosques worldwide, built by leading Muslim architects as well as designed by Western architects. Using photographs, the physical form of the mosque is explained. The development of the mosque and its architecture dependent upon the region's climatic factors, craft skills, and local building materials, are also examined in this excellent resource. Well-researched, it includes a bibliography, a glossary, and an index. "A welcome addition to the field of Islamic studies."—*Choice*

3 *Beauty and Islam: Aesthetics in Islamic Art and Architecture*
Gonzalez, Valerie.
London; New York: I. B. Tauris (in association with the Institute of Ismaili Studies in London), 2001. 134 pp.
ISBN: 1860646913
Grades 9–12
A series of lectures about Islamic art and architecture delivered at the Institute of Ismaili Studies in London is the basis of this text. Includes index and bibliographic references. Very informative. "Stimulating investigation of Islamic aesthetics."—*Choice*

4 *The Arts of Fire: Islamic Influences on Glass and Ceramics of the Italian Renaissance*
Hess, Catherine (editor) with contributions by Linda Komaroff and George Saliba.
Los Angeles: J. Paul Getty Museum, 2004. 172 pp.
ISBN: 0892367571; ISBN (pbk.): 089236758x
Grades 9–12
The reproductions of the art work, represented in striking color photographs, provide a visual feast for the eyes. Published to coincide with an exhibition at the famous J. Paul Getty Museum, this book demonstrates just

how important Islamic influences of the eighth and twelfth centuries were on the development of Italian luxury ceramics and glass. Essays by the editors demonstrate early modern Europe's debt to the Islamic world and help us get a better understanding of the interrelationships of cultures over time. Includes color photographs and illustrations, a glossary and references. Outstanding resource.

5 *What You Will See Inside a Mosque?*
Khan, Aisha Karen; photographs by Aaron Pepis.
Woodstock, Vermont. Skylight Paths Publishing, 2003. 31 pp.
ISBN: 1893361608
Grades 3–6
Designed to show various aspects of a traditional Muslim mosque, this book provides readers of all faiths the visual and informative introduction to the Muslim faith and worship. The book, which includes very effective photographs, is well recommended for children, teachers, parents and librarians who wish to understand people of various faiths.

6 *Portrait of Islam: A Journey through the Muslim World*
Laurance, Robin.
New York: Thames & Hudson, 2002. 168 pp.
ISBN: 0500510989
Grades 8–12
The 156 color photographs beautifully present a visual story of Islam from the areas of North and West Africa, Middle East, South Asia, and Southeast Asia. Robin Laurance, the photojournalist, has had his work published in a wide range of British and American publications. A stunning collection of photographs—"better than words" to illustrate Islam in specific regions of the world. The book also presents the principles of Islam, the tenets of the Islamic faith, and the relationship of Islam to Judaism and Christianity.

7 *The Buildings of Early Islam*
Leacroft, Helen and Richard Leacroft.
London: Hodder & Stoughton; Reading, Massachusetts: Addison-Wesley,
    1976. 40 pp.
ISBN: 0201094460
Grades 5–9
As people from several countries with different climates and types of building materials became followers of the Islamic religion, they built

mosques, schools, hospitals, and houses best suited to their needs. There were differences in the way these buildings were built; some were flat-roofed, some were domed, some were magnificent, and some were simple; however they all had the common necessary elements for the faith. The authors describe the famous Ka'bah, a shrine in the courtyard of the great mosque of Mecca toward which all Muslims turn five times a day in prayer. In addition to explaining the Prophet Muhammad's home and thatched rooms for his wives, the authors also explain the history and the architecture of other famous mosques, palaces, houses, and hospitals which were built in countries such as Iraq, Turkey, Egypt, Spain, and more. Includes some color and some black-and-white illustrations and maps as well as an index. An interesting resource to learn about Islamic contributions to architecture.

8 *Mosque*
Macaulay, David.
Boston: Houghton Mifflin Co., 2003. 96 pp.
ISBN: 2003000177
Grades 4–7
The author reveals the methods and materials used to design and construct a mosque in late-sixteenth-century Turkey. Through the fictional story and the illustrations, readers will learn not only how such monumental structures were built, but also how they functioned in relation to the society they served. The text and the detailed illustrations in this book complement each other. Includes a very helpful glossary.

9 *A 16th Century Mosque*
Macdonald, Fiona and Mark Bergin.
New York: P. Bedrick Books, 1994.
ISBN: 087226310X
Grades 9–12
Readers of this book will learn how mosques, the architecture, building techniques, and artistry in the sixteenth century influenced the lives of the Islamic people. The author also discusses briefly the history regarding the spread of Islam and the Islamic faith. Includes color illustrations, a glossary, and the Islamic calendar. Very informative and well organized. Recommended for school library collection.

10 *Islamic Art and Spirituality*
Nasr, Seyyed Hossein.
Albany, New York: State University of New York Press, 1987. 213 pp.

ISBN: 0887061745; ISBN (pbk.): 0887061753
Grades 11–12

Certain aspects of Islamic art from the point of view of Islamic spirituality and in relation to the principles of Islamic revelation are addressed in this book, which is primarily for the general reader as opposed to the specialist of Islamic art. The emphasis is mostly on Persian art, discussing calligraphy, painting, architecture, literature, music, and the plastic arts. The author explains how art plays a role in the life of individual Muslims and the community as a whole. The Sufi tradition within Islam is given an especially close look for its spiritual significance of beauty. Includes color illustrations and an index.

11 *Palace and Mosque: Islamic Art from the Middle East*
Stanley, Tom; Mariam Rosser-Owen, Stephen Vernoit.
London: Victoria & Art Publications, 2004. 144 pp.
ISBN: 0810965623
Grade 12

An outstanding resource that describes some of the magnificent art works produced in the Muslim world since the seventh century AD. This book offers an understanding of the wealth and sophistication of Islamic culture to large interested audiences around the world. The artistic work in this book is a testimony of the talent of its makers, and it demonstrates how, during this period, the Middle East retained a central place in the world. Includes a foreword by the Director of Victoria and Albert Museum, and an index. Illustrated with stunning impressionistic color photographs.

12 *The Story of Islamic Architecture*
Yeomans, Richard.
New York: New York University Press, 2000. 240 pp.
ISBN: 081479694x
Grade 12

This book draws attention to the best-known monuments and the mainstream of Islamic achievement. The author explains the architecture within a historical framework, and he relates it to the wider religious, social, and cultural context. In addition to discussing the religious basis of form and function in Islamic architecture, the author presents Ottoman, Egyptian, Spanish, Moroccan, Persian, and South Asian architecture. Includes a map, a selected bibliography, an index, and very striking color photographs. It is a very useful resource for those who wish to have an understanding of the significance of Islamic architecture.

2

Biographies

This chapter covers two subsections: The subsection "Muhammad," which predominantly covers the Prophet Muhammad's life contains six entries: one for high school, two for middle school, and three for elementary school grade levels. The second subsection under "Others" has thirteen entries, and it portrays biographies of heroes and personalities of the Muslim world who have contributed significantly to Islamic history and heritage. This subsection contains two resources for high school, four for middle school, and seven for elementary grade levels. There is a scarcity of materials available for grades K–3 in both subsections.

MUHAMMAD

13 *The Life of the Prophet Muhammad*
Azzam, Leila and Aisha Gouverneur; illustrations by Mary Hampson
    Minifie.
London: Islamic Texts Society, 1985. 135 pp.
ISBN: 0946621012; ISBN (pbk.): 0946621020
Grades 6–8
    This biography of Prophet Muhammad provides children with a necessary educational and cultural background about him in a very interesting manner. The prophet's family tree, the list of the prophet's wives, and the glossary deliver very useful information. Includes colored illustrations.

14 *Muhammad*
Demi.

New York: Margaret K. McElderry Books, 2003.
ISBN: 0689852649
Grades 2–4

Written by one of the award-winning creators of numerous books for
children, this is an excellent book that presents an account of the life and
mission of Prophet Muhammad. A great resource for those beginners who
wish to understand Islam. It is an enjoyable book. The author clarifies pre-
vailing misconceptions about Islam and the Prophet. Quotes from the
Qur'an appear throughout the book. The color illustrations, which complement the text, are based on traditional Islamic resources. An inspirational
book. "Demi weaves together selections from the Qur'an and an overview
of Islam in this excellent retelling of the Prophet's life that combines beauty
and scholarship."—*Booklist*

15 *Muhammad: The Messenger of God*
Kelen, Betty.
Nashville, Tennessee: Thomas Nelson, Inc., 1975. 278 pp.
ISBN: 0840764405
Grades 6–12

Discusses the life of Muhammad, the founder of Islam, and the religion
and civilization that he influenced. Some of the topics discussed are:
Mecca, Medina, Pillars of Islam, and death of Muhammad. The appendix
includes the names of Muhammad's wives. A bibliography and an index are
also included.

16 *Muhammad of Mecca: Prophet of Islam*
Marston, Elsa.
New York: Franklin Watts, 2001. 128 pp.
ISBN: 0531203867; ISBN (pbk.): 0531155544
Grades 5–9

This is a biography of Prophet Muhammad, the founder of the Muslim
religion. Basic information on Muslim beliefs and practices, and a brief history of Islam after Prophet Muhammad's death are also discussed. Contains
bibliographical references and index, including black-and-white illustrations. "This book is a useful addition to libraries, particularly those seeking
to expand their holdings on world religions."—*School Library Journal*

17 *Muhammad and Islam*
Merchant, Kerena.
Mankato, Minnesota: Smart Apple Media, 2003. 48 pp.

ISBN: 1583402179
Grades 3–5

This book is a brief introduction to the life of Muhammad that describes who he was, what he did, how he received Allah's messages, what he taught his followers. In addition, this book has a wealth of information about sacred places, festivals, the Qur'an, and the importance of Muhammad's teaching. Includes very effective colored pictures, a map of Saudi Arabia, a glossary, an index, and a list of additional resources. It is a very interesting book.

18 *Mohammed: Prophet of the Religion of Islam*
Pike, Royston.
New York: F. A. Praeger, 1969. 117 pp.
Grades 10–12

The author discusses the biography of the founder of Islam, who is considered by his followers as the first prophet of Allah. Muhammad could not read nor write, but his followers recorded his revelations in the Qur'an. The chapters in this book explain: the Qur'an, what a Muslim believes, and how he practices his faith. Includes black-and-white map, photographs, and an index. It is an interesting and very informative source.

OTHERS

19 *Hashim, Son of Abdu Munaaf*
Takoma Park, Maryland: The Muslim Students' Association of the United
    States and Canada, 1973. [16] pp.
Grades 2–4

Part of the Prophet's biography series for children, this small book relates the story of Amr, the Chief of the Quraysh tribe of Mecca. The people of Mecca named him Hashim after he gave them food and sustenance during a period of famine. Hashim also happened to be the grandfather of the Prophet Muhammad. Includes sketches and a map.

20 *Portraits of the Lives of the Successors to the Companions of Prophet
    Muhammad*
Al-Basha, Abdur Rahman; translated by Alexandra S. Al-Osh.
Fairfax, Virginia: Institute of Islamic and Arabic Sciences in America, Research Center, 1997. 3 volumes.
ISBN: 1569230463; ISBN (pbk.): 1569230471, 1569230498
Grades 6–8

This three-volume set discusses the stories of twelve prominent men (successors) who are models for those who practice Islam. These men (successors) learned their faith and values from men who were companions to the Prophet Muhammad. These volumes would provide inspiration to Muslim readers.

21 *Muslim Heroes of the World*
Atiqul, Haque M.
London: Ta-Ha, 1995. 140 pp.
ISBN: 1897940335
Grades 11–12
Heroes and personalities of the Muslim world who have contributed significantly to Islamic history and Islamic heritage are presented in this book. This book is translated from the book titled *Muslim Manisha* (Muslim heroes) written in the Bengali language by Justice Abdul Maudood. It covers biographies of twenty-nine individuals.

22 *So Many Enemies, So Little Time: An American Woman in All the Wrong Places*
Burkett, Elinor.
New York: HarperCollins Publishers, 2004. 325 pp.
ISBN: 0780635353
Grades 11–12
An American Fulbright professor presents her biography and a true adventurous story of her travels. She is accompanied by her husband to Kyrgyzstan in the heart of Central Asia. During her teaching assignment in Bishket, she and her husband encounter struggles with people who were used to living under Soviet rule. The couple then travel to Afghanistan after the fall of the Taliban, and to Iran, Iraq (before the fall of Sudan), Mongolia, Uzbekistan, China, Vietnam, Turkmenistan, Cambodia, Mongolia, and Myanamar. Many of these countries were not "friends" of the United States. The book would have been more interesting if it had pictures dispersed throughout the book. It is a useful source for educators who plan to teach in Muslim-dominated countries, particularly in Central Asia.

23 *Ayatollah Khomeini*
Gordon, Mathew.
New York: Chelsea House Publishers, 1976. 116 pp.
ISBN: 0877545596
Grades 6–9

The author presents this well-illustrated biography of Ayatollah Khomeini, a famous Shi'ite religious leader from Iran who became the chief political figure in Iran after the overthrow of the Shah in 1979. Since the author has woven historical background into the biographical information, this book is recommended for students with advanced reading skills. Includes black-and-white illustrations and an index. It is a well-researched book.

24 *Champion: The Story of Muhammad Ali*
Haskins, James; illustrations by Eric Velasquez.
New York: Walker & Co., 2002. (Unpaged.)
ISBN: 0802787843
Grades 3–5
Discusses Ali's boyhood in racially segregated Louisville, Kentucky, where, as Cassius Clay, he was introduced to boxing when he was twelve, and soon demonstrated talent at this game. The author also discusses Ali's retirement, his decision to join the Nation of Islam, his opposition to the Vietnam War, and his struggle with Parkinson's disease. Includes color illustrations. "Informative and inspiring." — *Publisher's Weekly*

25 *Tell Me about the Prophet Musa*
Khan, Saniyasnain; illustrated by K. M. Ravindran.
New Delhi: Goodword Books, 2001. 53 pp.
ISBN: 8187570482
Grades 6–8
In addition to the life of the Prophet Musa which was full of happenings, adventures, and excitement, the focus of this book is on the lessons for our daily lives. Beautifully illustrated, this book presents exciting historical events in a simple and informative style.

26 *Iqbal Masih and the Crusaders against Child Slavery*
Kuklin, Susan.
New York: H. Holt and Co., 1998. 133 pp.
ISBN: 0805054596
Grades 7–12
This is the story of Iqbal Masih, the former Pakistani child labor activist and spokesperson, who had been a slave himself and worked twelve-hour days in a Pakistani carpet factory. At the age of 13 he was murdered by people who felt threatened by his struggle for the rights of children. Though he was gone, his actions inspired an international awareness of child abuse and child labor. The book includes an index, a bibliography, a glossary and a pronunciation guide, and black-and-white photographs of children and labor

leaders. An appendix provides addresses of organizations to help readers learn more about child labor. In the year 2000, the first World's Children's Prize was awarded posthumously to Iqbal. The Prize also bears a text that pays tribute to Iqbal's memory: "The Iqbal Masih Award for the Rights of the Child." It is an excellent book. "Kuklin's gripping story complements and adds human interest to Jane Springer's *Listen to Us: The World's Working Children* (Groundwood, 1997), which draws on UNICEF documents and materials. Together they provide excellent coverage for discussion of this tragic problem."—*School Library Journal*

27 *Osama bin Laden: A War against the West*
Landau, Elaine.
Brookfield, Connecticut: Twenty-First Century Books, 2002. 144 pp.
ISBN: 0761317090
Grades 8–10
    This is a carefully researched book which traces Osama bin Laden's life, his movement to the forefront of an international terrorist network, and extremist views held by him and his followers that set them apart from the majority of Muslims around the world. In addition, the threat of terrorism that has been imposed on the world by Osama bin Laden is also discussed. Includes black-and-white photographs, a list of books for "further reading," an index, and a glossary. "Supplemented by a regularly updated website such as the one associated with PBS *Frontline*'s 'Hunting bin Laden,' this book may help students toward some understanding of the origins and motives of international terrorism."—*School Library Journal*

28 *Osama bin Laden*
Loehfelm, Bill.
San Diego, California: Lucent Books, 2003. 112 pp.
ISBN: 1590182944
Grades 6–8
    This is a well-researched, detailed biography of the founder of al-Qaeda, Osama bin Laden, which has been written in an objective and unbiased way. Excellent information boxes are provided separately to the bibliographical account to enhance the understanding of historical events that affected bin Laden's life. Includes a bibliography, a glossary, black-and-white photographs, maps, a chronology, and an index. Highly recommended for school libraries.

29 *Heroes and Holy Places*
Marcovitz, Hal.

Broomall, Pennsylvania: Mason Crest Publishers, 2004. 120 pp.
ISBN: 1590847040
Grades 6–9

This book provides short biographies of heroes, men and women, in the history of Islam, from its seventh-century beginnings to the late twentieth century. These individuals represent various ethnic and cultural groups, reflecting the diversity of the Muslim community of believers. The final chapter in this book focuses on the holiest cities of Islam, including Mecca, Medina, and Jerusalem, and explains why these places are revered by Muslims. It is a well-researched and richly informative book. It contains a chronology, Internet resources, an index, and color photographs. Highly recommended.

30 *Richard the Lionheart and the Third Crusade: The English King Confronts Saladin, AD 1191*
Power, Rhoda D.
London; New York: Putnam, 1931. 184 pp.
ISBN: 0823942139
Grades 5–8

Presents the historical background of the people as well as politics leading up to the Third Crusade, which involved the English King Richard I. It also chronicles the events of the Third Crusade, and the many battles between the Muslims and the crusaders. Provides middle-school children an introduction to Richard the Lionheart and the Crusades. Includes a bibliography, a glossary, an index, and color illustrations.

31 *Saladin: Noble Prince of Islam*
Stanley, Diane.
New York: HarperCollins Publishers, 2002. [45] pp.
ISBN: 0688171354
Grades 4–8

This is a story about Saladin, an extraordinary leader in Islam, who was known for his generosity, compassion, tolerance, and wisdom. He united his people and fought a war against the crusaders during the twelfth century. The detailed illustrations inspired by the Islamic art of the time are magnificent. Includes a bibliography and a glossary. The author is the recipient of the Orbis Pictus Award for Outstanding Nonfiction for Children. "Countless details of dress, armor, domestic interiors, and landscape evoke the period and setting. The beauty and sophistication of Islamic culture shine through Stanley's glorious pictures."—*School Library Journal*

3

Curricular Resources

This chapter contains fifty resources for teachers, parents, and librarians to develop lesson plans. Some of them are followed by class activities that could be modified according to grade levels—seven for high school, three for middle school, and forty for elementary school. Several of these entries are wonderful tools that provide religious education and culture for Muslim students. Some of the resources lend themselves to independent research. The majority of the resources are designed for Muslim children.

32 *Teaching about Islam and Muslims in the Public School Classroom: Handbook for Educators. 2nd ed.*
Fountain Valley, California: Council on Islamic Education, 1993. 97 pp.
ISBN: 1930109008
Grades 4–6
An excellent resource for teachers, parents, and librarians. This second edition differs from the third edition in that it lists educational resources for teaching about Islam and Muslims, which include "suggested activities for teaching about Islam and Muslims." These resources are divided into four categories: informational handouts for students to supplement textbooks and other materials, activity sheets for students grouped according to specific subject areas, suggested activities for teaching about Islam, and recommended books and videotapes.

33 *What Do We Say? (A Guide to Islamic Manners)*
Abdullah, Noorah Kathryn.
Leicester, England: Islamic Foundation, 1996. 24 pp.
ISBN: 0860372669
Grades K–1

A wonderful book for teaching children Islamic morals and etiquette. The color pictures help to reinforce the Islamic words. Recommended particularly for Muslim children. Includes glossary.

34 *The Crusades from Medieval European and Muslim Perspectives: A Unit of Study for Grades 7–12*
Aghaie, Kamran Scot.
Los Angeles: Council on Islamic Education and National Center for History in the Schools, University of California, Los Angeles. 1998. 76 pp.
Grades 7–12
This book contains materials for teachers and students to provide an understanding of cultural, religious, and military interaction between crusaders and Muslims. The five lesson plans include a variety of ideas and approaches for the teacher. Teaching units are based on primary sources taken from documents, artifacts, journals, diaries, newspapers, and literature from the period under study. A bibliography and a list of web resources are included.

35 *Muslim Women through the Centuries: A Unit of Study for Grades 7–12*
Aghaie, Kamran Scot; Munir A. Shaikh.
Los Angeles: Council on Islamic Education, National Center for History in the Schools, 1998. 51 pp.
Grades 7–12
The purpose of the four units covered in this book is to explore issues relating to women in Islam as well as women in Muslim history. The units are: women's rights and protections in Islam, gender roles and women's identities in Muslim society, Muslim women leaders through the centuries and famous Muslim women as role models. Each unit includes materials for teachers and lesson plans with student resources. A very useful resource guide for teachers.

36 *The Children's Book of Islam: Part One*
Ahsan, Muhammad Manazir.
Leicester, England: The Islamic Foundation, 1979. 56 pp.
ISBN: 0950395412; ISBN (pbk.): 0860370372
Grades 2–3
This book (part one) is intended to be used as a basic textbook on the fundamentals of Islamic faith for the younger generation of the Muslims living in Europe and other parts of the world. The "workbook" containing ques-

tions is a very useful part of this book. Includes black-and-white pictures. It has also been published in French, German, and Dutch.

37 *The Children's Book of Islam: Part Two*
Ahsan, Muhammad Manazir.
Leicester, England: Islamic Foundation, 1993. 64 pp.
ISBN: 0860370372
Grades 3–5
  Part two of this book expands on the core precepts of Islam introduced previously in part one. A wonderful educational tool that provides Islamic religious education to young Muslim students, particularly living in a culture different from Islam. It discusses the Five Pillars of Islam and also includes a very useful "workbook" of questions.

38 *The Islamic Year: Surahs, Stories and Celebrations*
Al-Gailani, Noorah and Chris Smith; illustrated by Helen Williams.
Stroud, Gloucestershire, England: Hawthorn Press, 2002. 218 pp.
ISBN: 1903458145
Grades 4–7
  Beautifully illustrated, with Arabic calligraphy of the names of God, traditional patterns, maps and pictures drawn from many parts of the Muslim world, this book tells the story of the Prophet Muhammad in an engaging manner. The Muslim festivals are explained in a simple and clear way through stories, songs, games, recipes, craft and art activities. An excellent resource for those educators who are seeking to interpret Islam to non-Muslim audiences. In addition to "references and further reading" the book includes a very helpful appendix listing "suggestions for teachers." "Not just for Muslims, this book offers helpful and accessible information for non-Muslim educators and parents who are interested in interfaith understanding."—*Publishers Weekly*

39 *Allah is Al-Khaliq (The Creator)*
Ameen, Saba Ghazi.
Skokie, Illinois: IQRA International Education Foundation, 2002. 11 pp.
ISBN: 1563160706
Grades K–1
  An enchanting colorfully illustrated book for teaching colors by using positive Islamic themes in a simple manner that young children can relate to.

40 *Allah Is Ar-Rahman (the Compassionate)*
Ameen, Saba Ghazi.
Skokie, Illinois: IQRA International Educational Foundation, 2002.
ISBN: 1563160692
Grades K–1
   A unique book with images that can be reproduced to teach preschool concepts pertaining to colors, letters, shapes, and numbers by stressing positive Islamic themes. A wonderful read-aloud book.

41 *Islam*
Arquilevich, Gabriel.
Westminster, California: Teacher Created Materials, 2002. 48 pp.
ISBN: 0743936809
Grades 4–6
   Religious studies foster tolerance. This book is a very important resource for teachers to use as they work to provide students essential knowledge regarding Islam. Lessons focus on: the life of Muhammad, the Qur'an, Pillars of Islam, after Muhammad, places of worship, rites of passage, symbols of Islam, Islam today, art of writing, and vocabulary. The book has a cumulative review section containing quiz, followed by the answer key. Includes some maps and black-and-white illustrations. It is a well-organized book, and is highly recommended for teachers.

42 *World Religions: Interdisciplinary Unit: Challenging*
Arquilevich, Gabriel.
Huntington Beach, California: Teacher Created Materials, 1995. 288 pp.
ISBN: 1557346240
Grades 6–8
   This book is divided into two sections: 1. Semitic religions of Judaism, Christianity, and Islam. 2. Indian religions of Hinduism, Buddhism, and Sikhism. These are supplemented by a chapter on Taoism. Each chapter focuses on one religion, and discusses its origin, worship and prayer, calendar, basic teachings, sacred text, places of worship and pilgrimage, and holidays and festivals, followed by a review and a quiz. An additional chapter discusses atheism and agnosticism. The final chapter is activity based, dedicated to comparison and reflection. It is an excellent resource for the study of various religions. Students will also have an opportunity to do independent research before answering some of the questions. Includes black-and-

white maps, illustrations, a bibliography, and an answer key to the questions listed at the end of each chapter. Highly recommended for teachers and parents.

43 *The Brave Elephant*
Aygun, Aysegul; translated by Hakan Yesilova; illustrated by Lojistik Art.
Rutherford, New Jersey: Light, 2002. 24 pp.
ISBN: 1932099018
Grades 1–3
During their travel together in search of water, a giant elephant shares with the little squirrel his story about helping defeat the enemies of Allah. This is a story mentioned in the Holy Qur'an's Chapter of the Elephant. The text is complemented with striking color illustrations. The book includes nine questions for discussion purposes.

44 *Muslim Manners: A Guide for Parents and Educators of Muslim Children*
Azami, Iqbal Ahmad.
Leicester, England: UK Islamic Academy, 1990. 93 pp.
ISBN: 1872531083
Grades 5–8
A comprehensive guide to traditional Islamic teaching and its effect on Muslims' daily lives covers topics such as human kindness, rights and duties, truth and falsehood, habits, promoting unity and other virtues. Each chapter is followed by a set of questions which should be very helpful in ensuring that students fully understand the Islamic teaching regarding each subject. Although this book is aimed at 11–14-year-old children, parents and teachers of younger children will find it an equally useful tool to strengthen positive attitudes toward Islamic-oriented behavior.

45 *National Security*
Bhattacharjee, Anjali.
Farmington Hills, Michigan: Gale Group, 2003. 202 pp.
ISBN: 0787665460
Grades 11–12
Various aspects of U.S. national security are presented in ten chapters and three indexes of this book. Each chapter begins with an overview of the basic facts and background information regarding the threat of conventional weapons; proliferation of weapons of mass destruction; preparing for biological and chemical attacks; international terrorism; domestic

terrorism; civilian national security infrastructure; the military, peace-keeping, and national security; global dynamics of national security; alliances and resources; new arenas; organized crime and emerging technologies. Includes indexes, tables, charts, and graphs to illustrate facts and figures. This is an ideal resource that can be used for class assignments, reports, and research projects by honor students.

46 *Women in Islam: The Ancient Middle East to Modern Times*
Bingham, Marjorie Wall; Susan Hill Gross.
Hudson, Wisconsin: G. E. McCuen Publications, 1980. 129 pp.
ISBN: 0865960259; ISBN (pbk.): 0865960003
Grades 10–12
Part of the series "Women in World Cultures," this is the product of a federally funded grant to develop materials on women for global studies and world history courses. This book presents historical roles of Muslim women and information on their contemporary status, and provides students with some resources for discovering the diversity of women's roles in Islam. Descriptions by women of their own lives have been used whenever possible. Additional information is provided using government reports, statistics, anthropologists' data, folklore, and art; however, the statistics are outdated since they were reported in 1980. The book contains six chapters: women in the ancient Middle East, women in early Islam, four aspects of the Islamic view of women, separate worlds, a diversity of roles, and women in the modern Middle East. "Points to consider" at the end of each unit within every chapter should be very helpful for classroom discussion and for further research on the subject. Includes black-and-white illustrations, maps, a glossary of terms and a bibliography.

47 *Masajid Allah*
Biscevic, Samir and S. Azmath Al. Khan.
Chicago: IQRA Book Center, 1999. 31 pp.
Grades K–1
Although this is a coloring book, it is also a wonderful educational tool for teaching the architecture of famous mosques around the world.

48 *Ali Baba and the 40 Thieves*
Casper; illustrated by Domenec Blade.
Barcelona: Didaco, 1996. 1 v. unpaged + 1 sound cassette.
ISBN: 8489712204
Grades 2–3

Beautifully illustrated in color, this book is about Ali Baba's discovery of a group of thieves' hidden treasure. The accompanying sound cassette is a very useful tool for learning the pronunciation of the words in the text.

49 *We are Muslim Children: Songs and Verses for Muslim Girls and Boys*
Chaudhry, Saida.
Indianapolis, Indiana: American Trust Publications, 1993. 49 pp.
ISBN: 0892591269; ISBN (pbk.): 0892590505
Grades 2–4
The author compiled this book especially for the Muslim children of the North American continent in mind. The Islamic way of life and Islamic values are described through songs and verses. Includes a very helpful section for teachers and parents, titled, "How to Sing the Action Songs and Play the Games." It is recommended that the songs be sung to tunes performed on the accompanying tape. Also included are color illustrations.

50 *Symbols of Islam*
Chebel, Malek; photographs by Laziz Hamani.
New York: Assouline Publishing, 1999. 127 pp.
ISBN: 284323199x
Grades K–5
Through color pictures and clear text, the author thoroughly explains the symbols of Islam. It provides a visual synthesis of the Islamic world. Includes a glossary and bibliographical references.

51 *Threads of Time: Junior World History 400–1750*
Coupe, Sheena M. and Barbara Scanlan.
Melbourne, Australia: Longman Cheshire, 1986. 256 pp.
ISBN: 0582663423; ISBN (pbk.): 0201746697
Grades 9–12
Topics in world history from the fall of the Roman Empire to the mid-eighteenth century are surveyed in this book. The author provides students with an understanding of the history of cultures from various parts of the world, including Europe, the Arab world, Asia, and the Americas. Whenever appropriate, major developments that brought about change are discussed. In addition, various cultures are compared and contrasted. This book offers an integrated skills and knowledge approach. Sections "Time to Understand" and "How Do We Know" at the end of each of the fourteen chapters will help develop historical knowledge of students. It consists of a wealth of written and pictorial material. Includes color and some

black-and-white illustrations, and an index. Highly recommended, particularly for follow-up discussions regarding each topic.

52 *Learning about Islam*
Emerick, Yahiya.
New York: IBTS, 1998. 211 pp.
ISBN: 1889720194
Grades 3–6

An extensive collection of informative readings, designed to meet younger children's need for Islamic education. The units are about Islamic beliefs, teachings, and practices as well as various aspects pertaining to Muslim-oriented art and civilization. Pre-reading and follow-up activities for each story with review exercises at the end of each unit should be very helpful for lesson planning for teachers. Recommended particularly for Muslim schools; however, it can be equally useful to anyone interested in learning about Islam. Includes a map, illustrations, and an index.

53 *What Islam is all about: student textbook*
Emerick, Yahiya.
Long Island City, New York: International Books & Tapes Supply, 1997.
    403 pp.
ISBN: 1889720380; ISBN (pbk.): 1889720372
Grades 9–12

The eighteen units in this text cover the basic history of the Prophet Muhammad, the teachings of Islam, the history of the ancient Prophets, the study of the Qur'an, the Islamic philosophy of the world and life within, Islamic law, Hadith and contemporary issues. Every unit has review exercises and questions. Contains index. Recommended for school library collections.

54 *We are Muslim, Al-Hamdu Lillah*
Fannoun, Kathy.
Chicago: IQRA International Educational Foundation, 1994. 1 v. (unpaged)
ISBN: 1563163195
Grades K–1

Discusses the universality of Islam and equality of human beings. Great book for activity lessons. Teachers may read these verses to the children, help them memorize and recite together in unison, and/or dress up as the children representing different Islamic countries of the world, and sing together. Great color illustrations showing diversity of Muslim children from various countries around the world are included.

55 *Teachings of the Qur'an, volume 3*
Ghazi, Abid U. and Tasneema Khatoon Ghazi.
Chicago: IQRA International Educational Foundation, 1996.
ISBN: 1563161133; ISBN (pbk.): 156316101x
Grades 4–7
Designed to represent the first systematic attempt to introduce the message of the Qur'an to children of elementary and junior grades at their own level of comprehension and understanding. It is divided into three sections pertaining to the Qur'an, namely human community, Muslim community, and social action. Includes an appendix, a glossary, and exercises to reinforce the general theme of the Qur'an and new and difficult words.

56 *A True Promise*
Ghazi, Abidullah and Tasneema Ghazi; illustrated by Mike Rezac.
Chicago: IQRA International Educational Foundation, 1992. 25 pp.
ISBN: 1563163047
Grades 3–6
The values conveyed in the eight stories of this book are universal, and could be taught to children of any generation and any religion. These values will help readers relate to others with patience, compassion, love, and understanding. These stories could also be acted out in the classroom. Includes illustrations.

57 *My Coloring Book of Salah*
Ghazi, Dr. Abidullah al-Ansari.
Skokie, Illinois: IQRA International Educational Foundation, 1994. 30 pp.
ISBN: 1563160528
Grades K–2
The focus of this book is the five religious prayers in Islam and the proper ways to administer them. A fun activity for young children.

58 *Eleven Surahs Explained*
Hashim, A. S.
Brentwood, Maryland: International Graphics Printing Service, 1990. 85 pp.
ISBN: 0686184122
Grades 5–10
In this third edition, eleven short chapters from the Qur'an, called surahs, are written in the Arabic language and are translated into English. Each part of the surah is explained briefly. The end of the whole surah is followed by questions and vocabulary. Since teaching these surahs is a fundamental

necessity for Muslims, it can be a part of the curriculum of any Islamic study. This will also be a step forward toward being able to read the Qur'an in Arabic.

59 *My Little Book about Allah*
Hussaini, Mohammad Mazhar.
Bolingbrook, Illinois: Al-Meezan International, Inc. 68 pp.
ISBN: 0911119280
Grades 5–8
   Although this book is organized with the young reader in mind, it is a useful resource for parents and teachers of Muslim children. Each of the seventeen chapters has a "Key Words" section, which lists important words in alphabetical order. In the body of the text, the names of Allah are presented in Arabic language, along with the transliterations, translations, and explanations of the attributes. Practical application of the attributes of Allah are set forth in the section called "Applying Knowledge." Each chapter includes a "Review" section followed by an activity.

60 *My Little Book about the Qur'an*
Hussaini, Mohammad Mazhar.
Bolingbrook, Illinois: Al-Meezan International, 1990. 62 pp.
ISBN: 0911119272
Grades 1–5
   Written especially for Muslim children, the main objectives of this book are to introduce children to the Qur'an; to provide factual information about the purpose, significance, and relevance of the Qur'an to their lives; to stimulate children to read the Qur'an; and to motivate children to act upon the message of the Qur'an. Each of the twenty-four chapters begins with key words and their definitions, followed by the main body of the chapter. The final section in each chapter is titled "Think and Answer," which allows children to get actively involved in processing the information presented. A very useful teaching guide for Muslim parents and teachers.

61 *A is for Allah*
Islam, Yusuf.
London: Mountain of Light, 2000. 63 pp. + 2 sound cassettes.
ISBN: 1900675315; ISBN (pbk.): 1900675277 (with double cassettes/CDs)
Grades 2–5
   Using the same title as his song, Yusuf Islam, the famous pop star in the '60s and the '70s, formerly known as Cat Stevens, introduces the Ara-

bic alphabet in this book. He teaches that the letter A stands first and foremost for Allah the Almighty, and not only for Apple, as commonly taught. Each letter of the alphabet is presented with striking color illustrations. The text is mostly in English but includes Arabic vocabulary. Songs on the two accompanying cassettes/CDs are sung primarily in English, and are very enjoyable.

62 *My Book of Islam*
Kay, Friesen (editor); illustrated by Khalid Dow.
Ottawa, Canada: Council of Muslim Communities of Canada, 1988.
ISBN: 0886280184
Grades 2–9
Provides basic information on Islam. Material for the text was reviewed by many Muslim organizations, schoolteachers, imams, and students. It has a "teacher's guide" with recommended lesson presentations and questions pertaining to each of the seven chapters containing thirty lessons. The topics covered in this text are the Qur'an, beliefs, Ibadat, Prophet Muhammad's life, stories from the Qur'an, conduct and behavior, and Muslim countries.

63 *Id-ul-Fitr*
Kerven, Rosalind
Austin, Texas: Raintree Steck-Vaughn, 1997. 31 pp.
ISBN: 0817246096
Grades 2–3
From the "World of Holidays" series, this book discusses the celebration of Id al-Fitr, the holiday at the end of Ramadan—a month of fasting. The lively text and very attractive color photographs and art reproductions demonstrate how a Muslim family spends the day of Id al-Fitr, beginning in the morning when the whole family dresses in their best clothes, goes to mosque for prayers, feasts, and participates in fun and fair. The Five Pillars of Islam are explained in a brief, simplified way. The author has included some activities for young children to enjoy, such as making a pudding, and making an identification card. A glossary, books for "further reading," and an index are included. Highly recommended.

64 *Muslim Child: Understanding Islam through Stories and Poems*
Khan, Rukhsana; illustrated by Patty Gallinger.
Morton Grove, Illinois: Albert Whitman & Co., 2002. 104 pp.
ISBN: 0807553077
Grades 3–7

This very well-written book is a child-centered introduction to Islam. Using stories and poems of children from various countries, including the United States, Canada, Pakistan, and Nigeria, the author provides insight into a way of life that is often misunderstood by people in the West. Black-and-white illustrations and follow-up activity lessons for children are included. Also included in the book is a very helpful "pronunciation guide" that represents a rough transliteration of the Arabic terms used in the stories. Recommended for the elementary school library collection. "In a time when non-Muslim children are likely to be asking questions about Islam, this book does have some answers, and its scenarios can serve as springboards for discussion about Islam and religious tolerance." — *Booklist*

65 *Qur'an Stories for Kids*
Khan, Saniyasnian; illustrated by Achla Anand and K. Anand.
Goodword Books, 2002.
Grades 3–5
These best-loved twelve tales from the Qur'an provide a foundation on which to build a growing knowledge of the scriptures. The enjoyable tales are easy to read and to understand. The color illustrations complement the text. Each of the twelve tales is accompanied by a coloring book.

66 *Stories from the Muslim World*
Khattab, Huda; illustrated by Robert Geary.
London: Ta-Ha, 1996. 44 pp.
ISBN: 1897940343
Grades 5–8
This second revised edition is a collection of marvelous short stories, complemented by color illustrations as page borders. The stories are organized under chapter headings, namely, the beginnings of Islam, Muslims in history, and Muslim tales. The last section of the book contains a quiz containing thirty-one questions for reading comprehension, followed by answers.

67 *ABC Rhymes for Young Muslims*
Kishta, Leila.
Indianapolis, Indiana: American Trust Publications, 1984. 32 pp.
ISBN: 0892590440
Grades K–2
This book is an attempt to interest young children in Islam by using verses for each of the English alphabet letters. It contains catchy verses,

phrases, songs, and color alphabet letters which make the text appealing to young children. Although designed mostly for young Muslim children, non-Muslim children will also enjoy this book.

68 *My Muslim Faith*
Knight, Khadijah.
London: Evans, 1998. 30 pp.
ISBN: 0237518988
Grades 1–2
Using beautiful color photographs and simple text, the author discusses topics which are very important in the Muslim faith, such as prayers, the Ka'bah, the Qur'an, the Prophet Muhammad, Ramadan, the Hajj, Ramadan, and Id. Notes for teachers and parents provide extra information to help develop children's knowledge and understanding of the different Islamic beliefs and traditions. Includes a glossary and an index.

69 *The Islamic World: Beliefs and Civilizations, 600–1600*
Mantin, Peter and Ruth Mantin.
Cambridge, England; New York: Cambridge University Press, 1993, 64 pp.
ISBN: 0521406099
Grades 5–7
This is an excellent book that covers topics such as: what is Islam? The rise of Islam from 600–1600 AD, Islamic civilization and its influence, and Islam today. The authors provide teachers with the necessary material required to develop students' understanding of basic Islamic beliefs and historical knowledge regarding Islam. Each of the chapters has a list of very helpful thought-provoking questions for developing critical thinking and classroom discussion on the subject. Includes an index and an "Attainment Target Grid," a simple device to help teachers plan the study unit. Color illustrations complement the text. Highly recommended for teachers.

70 *Muslim Nursery Rhymes*
McDermott, Mustafa Yusuf; illustrations by Mary Clements.
Leicester, England: Islamic Foundation, 1981. 40 pp.
ISBN: 0860373428; ISBN (pbk.): 0860370755
Grades 2–3
A collection of fifteen nursery rhymes, accompanied by color illustrations, teaches young readers the meaning of life. Based on traditional English nursery rhymes, this collection makes children aware of Islamic values, and helps

develop a sense of self-confidence in young children. Should be of particular importance to Muslim children living in a multicultural environment. A book that should be fun to read, and should appeal to young children.

71 *Muslim Festival Tales*
Merchant, Kerena; illustrated by Tina Barber.
Austin, Texas: Raintree Steck-Vaughn, 2001. 32 pp.
ISBN: 0739827359
Grades 2–4
   The author focuses on the Muslim fasts and feasts using stories, poems, and prayers. The book contains a song children could dance to, a delicious snack that children could make, and a play that children would enjoy performing. A glossary, an index, and some useful resources are included. Beautifully illustrated.

72 *Grandma Hekmatt Remembers: An Arab-American Family Story*
Morris, Ann; photographs and illustrations by Peter Linenthal.
Brookfield, Connecticut: Millbrook Press, 2003. 30 pp.
ISBN: 0761328645; ISBN (pbk.): 0761319441
Grades 1–3
   Three Arab-American girls, Suzanne, Yasmine, and Sara, live with their parents in New Jersey. Their grandfather, Hedaiet, and grandmother, Hekmatt, who grew up in Cairo, Egypt, and moved to New Jersey, live nearby. The girls learn from their grandparents about Egypt, where Hekmatt and Hedaiet still return on vacations to visit family. They also learn about Arab culture, and how to write in Arabic. Includes a list of "special words," "family tree," and beautiful color photographs and illustrations. Includes directions for making Egyptian paper boats. An enjoyable activity lesson, included at the end of the book, would allow children to participate and learn about themselves and their heritage. An excellent book.

73 *Color and Learn Islamic Terms*
Qazi, M. A.
Chicago: Kazi Publications, 1985. 30 pp.
0935782249
Grades K–4
   A wonderful teaching tool for children to learn the Arabic language and the basics of Islam. It is one of a series of coloring books. The other three coloring books are: *Arabic Alphabets Coloring Book*; *Color and Learn Muslim Names*; and *Color and Learn Salat*. Recommended for Muslim children.

74 *Islam: A Very Short Introduction*
Ruthven, Malise.
New York: Oxford University Press, 2000. 157 pp.
ISBN: 0192853899
Grade 12
   Originally published in 1997, this is a 2000 revision that addresses major issues about Islam in regard to controversial issues and stereotypes. Ruthven introduces the reader to the basics of Islam, and also discusses the arguments in regard to fundamentalism. Questions pertaining to Jihad (Holy War), and major divisions among Islamic sects, such as the Shi'ite, the Sunni, and the Wahhabi, are addressed. This book provides a much needed discussion of the past, the present, and the future of Islam, and its place in other world religions. A helpful resource for upper grade levels for discussion and research. Black-and-white pictures complement the text. Includes an index.

75 *Ramadan Activities*
Salah, Comilita M.; Kathleen Kehl Lewis; illustrated by Ben DeSoto.
Westminster, California; Teacher Created Materials, Inc., 2000. 16 leaves.
ISBN: 1576906094
Grades 4–6
   An excellent book packed with all types of projects and ideas for learning and teaching about Ramadan, the holy month of fasting for Muslims. An overview of Islam and Ramadan is done, using creative activities and crafts, learning games, and extension activities and resources, which children should be able to enjoy. Answer keys are provided at the end of the book. Includes black-and-white illustrations. Recommended particularly for Muslim schools.

76 *Animals*
Sardar, Farah; illustrated by Vinah Ahluwalia.
Leicester, England: Islamic Foundation, 1997. (unpaged)
ISBN: 0860373371; ISBN (pbk.): 0860372685
Grades: K–1
   From the series titled, "Allah the Maker" this is a wonderful book that introduces the world of animals to children. It reinforces the wonders of Allah's creation. Color illustrations enhance the usefulness of this book.

77 *Islam for Younger People*
Sarwar, Ghulam.

London: Muslim Educational Trust, 1997. 64 pp.
ISBN: 0907261329
Grades 2–5

Written specifically for younger Muslim children living in an English-speaking country, this is an excellent reference book for teachers and parents to create a foundation to understand the religion of Islam. Includes illustrations and worksheets for children to complete.

78 *Teaching about Islam and Muslims in the Public School Classroom: Handbook for Educators. 3rd ed*
Shaikh, Munir A.
Fountain Valley, California: Council on Islamic Education, 1995. 117 pp.
ISBN: 1930109008
Grades 9–12

A highly recommended book for any middle and high school library. This third revised edition is an excellent resource for teachers, parents, and librarians who have a challenging task of teaching various important aspects of Islam and Muslims in an unbiased way. This handbook is a product of both a religious community and an educational community. It contains four equally important and critical sections: information on Islam; discussion of sensitive matters; a revised, comprehensive glossary of terms related to Islam with a pronunciation guide; and an updated annotated list of recommended books, video tapes, teaching resources, and reading materials for students. This third edition also includes topics and chapters that are not covered in the second edition.

79 *Muslim*
Tames, Richard.
Danbury, Connecticut: Children's Press, 1996. 32 pp.
ISBN: 0516080784; ISBN (pbk.): 0750239174
Grades 3–5

This excellent book from the series titled "Beliefs and Cultures" introduces children to the Muslim religion beginning with the teachings of the Prophet Muhammad, the beliefs of Islam, Islamic customs and practice. In addition, this book provides instructions to create symbolic Islamic crafts, such as making a book cover, a mosque, and a decorated plate. These craft activities, spotlight boxes, and interviews add new dimensions to learning about the people, culture, and history of Islam. Complemented by color photographs. Includes an index.

80 *The World of Islam: A Teacher's Handbook*
Tames, Richard.
London: Extramural Division, School of Oriental and African Studies
   (University of London), 1977. 229 pp.
ISBN: 0728600331
Grades 9–12
   Although published in 1977, this is a timeless book of specific topics in
regard to Islam with suggestions for introductory and survey courses. Since
the material is specific to Great Britain, it will need some modification in
order to be used for students in other countries. The chapters are: introduction to Islam, geography and environment, history, religious studies, and
social studies. Each chapter is followed by very interesting activities, discussion topics, suggested readings, and illustrations.

81 *Muslim Holidays*
Winchester, Faith.
Mankato, Minnesota: Bridgestone Books, 1999. 24 pp.
ISBN: 1560654597
Grades 1–3
   Beliefs of Muslims are discussed. In addition, seven of the special cele-
brations from the Islamic faith are also described. Contains an exercise for
a hands-on activity for children. Includes effective color illustrations. Ac-
companied by a teacher's guide.

4

Digital Electronic Resources

This chapter encompasses sixty-six entries, pertaining to various subjects. The entries included in this format are organized alphabetically under chapter headings similar to the ones in the print form. There are forty-seven entries for high school, fourteen for middle school, and five for elementary school grade levels. The advantage of the visual and audio materials is that they complement different learning styles. Some of the documentaries are recommended to be viewed in segments due to their length, and can be adapted for classroom use.

ART AND ARCHITECTURE

82 *Art and the Islamic World*
Washington, D.C.: Middle East Institute, 1993. 32 min., col.
Grades 9–12
   The art and architecture of mosques and buildings in various Islamic countries such as Morocco, Turkey, Iran, Egypt, Spain, Syria, and India, are discussed in this video. The viewers will enjoy numerous beautiful Islamic art and architecture works, for example, Persian miniature paintings of heroes and heroines, silk rugs, scientific drawings of plants and clocks, lamps, beautiful architecture used in Moghul buildings such as the Taj Mahal. In addition to the Islamic calligraphy, this documentary also explores the pottery, needlework, copper and brass-work, textile and carpet weaving developed in the Islamic countries a number of centuries ago. Western artists inspired by Islamic artifacts created works using Islamic techniques. Over the centuries, mosque architecture is retained but it also developed variations

related to local climate, building materials, customs, and artistic traditions. An excellent and invaluable documentary to provide information regarding Islamic art and architecture and its influence on the entire world.

83 *Islam, Empire of Faith*
Alexandria, Virginia: PBS Home Video, 2000. 2 videocassettes. (ca.180 min.), col.
ISBN: 0780635353
Grades 8–12

Academy award winner Ben Kingsley narrates the rise and growth of Islam throughout the world, since the birth of Prophet Muhammad in the sixth century through the peak of the Ottoman Empire under the reign of Suleyman the Magnificent one thousand years later. It also discusses the impact of Islamic civilization on world history and culture, the contributions and the impact that Muslims have made in art, education, trade, science, medicine, and philosophy. This documentary was screened by Muslim scholars, community leaders, and activists before it was aired on PBS. They defined this program as "a balanced and accurate portrayal of Islamic history." A must for junior and high school libraries.

84 *Islamic Art*
Princeton, New Jersey: Films for the Humanities, 1988. 30 min., col.
ISBN: 0891137025
Grades 11–12

The architecture and sculpture of mosques, fascinating calligraphy of sacred texts, the art of the garden, leather work, carpet making, and Islamic music are discussed in this program. In addition, the influence of abstract arabesque on Western art is covered in this video-recording. Should be of great interest to those who want to learn the background of Islamic art.

85 *Islamic Science and Technology*
Princeton, New Jersey: Films for the Humanities, 1988. 30 min., col.
ISBN: 0891137041
Grades 10–12

Part of the series "The World of Islam," this program explores how Arabic was the language of mathematics and science from the middle of the eighth century until the European Renaissance. It also explains how Islamic knowledge made very important contributions in the areas of astronomy, engineering, medicine, and physics.

86 *Miracles of the Qur'an*
IPCI Islamic vision; OKUR Production, 1990s. 65 min., col.
Grades 10–12
  Scientific facts described in the Qur'an, which have only been discovered by scientists during the twentieth century, are presented in this extraordinary documentary. Scientific truth revealed in the Qur'an pertain to astronomy, physics, and biology. This video also presents the unique style of the Qur'an, revealed fourteen centuries ago, and the superior wisdom it represents. A very interesting documentary.

87 *The Wonders of Islamic Science*
Chicago: Sound Vision, 1989. 30 min., col.
Grades 9–12
  Directed and narrated by Jawad Jafry, this fascinating documentary video discusses how the Qur'an inspired Muslims to lead the world in science and civilization. It describes the remarkable achievements of Muslims in various fields such as astronomy, mathematics, geography, botany, medicine, and zoology. Well recommended.

BIOGRAPHY

Muhammad

88 *Muhammad: Legacy of a Prophet*
Alexandria, Virginia: Unity Productions Foundation, 2002. 116 min., col.
ISBN: 0972628614
Grades 7–12
  An outstanding color presentation of the life of the Prophet Muhammad, who changed world history. In addition to showing film viewers the ancient Middle Eastern sites where Muhammad's life story began, the film also shows how some of the seven million Muslims' homes, mosques, and workplaces in North America continue to follow Prophet Muhammad's teachings. Highly recommended.

Others

89 *Osama Bin Laden: In the Name of Allah*
New York: A & E Home Video, 2002. Ca. 50 minutes; col. With black-and-white
ISBN: 0767051378
Grades 9–12

An exceptionally well-documented video, produced by ABC News Productions for A & E Networks, this biography traces the influences of people and events that shaped Osama bin Laden, one of the 50 children of bin Laden by his fourth official wife. The video also documents Osama bin Laden's hatred of the West and his influence to initiate acts of terrorism as the leader of al-Qaeda.

CURRICULAR RESOURCES

90 *Adam's World series* (14 videos)
Chicago: Sound Vision, 1991– . 30 minutes each, col.
Grades K–3
Directed by Jawad Jafry, the top-ranking Muslim director in North America, the Adam's World series includes the following titles: (1) Let's Pray. (2) Happy to Be a Muslim. (3) Finding Courage. (4) Take Me to the Kaba. (5) Kindness in Islam. (6) Thank You Allah. (7) Born to Learn. (8) Home Sweet Home. (9) Ramadan Mubarak. (10) The Humble Muslim. (11) One Big Family. (12) Zakat Helps Everyone. (13) Alif for Allah. (14) Adam's World. This unique Islamic video series for children introduces children to Islamic morals, concepts and behavior, values and culture in an educational and entertaining manner. Each video in the series also helps children learn Arabic letters and vocabulary with the help of puppets, animation, songs, and visits to Muslim countries. Many viewers call this program the "Muslim Sesame Street." One of the most highly recommended series for young Muslim children.

91 *Colors of Islam* [sound recording]
Chicago: Sound Vision, 2000.
Grades K–5
This is a compact disc with eight children's songs in English about Islam. Some Arabic language and phrases are used for introduction to songs. More appropriate for Muslim children.

92 *Islam in America*
Boston: Christian Science Monitor Video, 1992. 60 min. col.
Grades 6–12
Stereotypes and misconceptions of Muslims have been in existence in the United States and abroad for quite some time. This program helps viewers understand this religion. The video covers the Five Pillars of Islam, the basic requirements of faith for Muslims throughout the world. These Five

Pillars, as practiced in five American communities are discussed: "Faith" in Cedar Rapids, Iowa; "Prayer" in Los Angeles; "Charity" in Houston, Texas; "Fasting" in Quincy, Massachusetts; and "Pilgrimage" in Toledo, Ohio. A learning guide of eight pages is included, which can be used for discussion and activities after viewing the video. Very interesting.

93 *Islam*
Wynnewood, Pennsylvania: Schlessinger Media, 1998. 50 min. col.
ISBN: 1572252057
Grades 9–12
Narrated by Academy Award winner Ben Kingsley, this video explores Islam's history from its inception in the seventh century by Muhammad to the rise of the Ottoman Empire between the nineth and twelfth centuries and to the present. It also discusses the wealth of Islamic art, architecture, calligraphy and other contributions that made Islam an important influence in the twentieth century. Teacher's Guide is available online at libraryvideo.com. Discussion of the topic before and after viewing the video will allow an interesting dialogue for the students.

94 *Wearing Hijab: Uncovering the Myths of Islam in the United States*
Denver, Colorado: Auraria Media Center, 2003. 34 min., col. + 1 instructor's manual (53 pp.)
ISBN: 0736589244
Grades 11–12
In the United States, there are many misconceptions about Islam, particularly when it comes to its distinctive veil, known as hijab. How do Muslim women in this country feel about wearing a hijab? In this documentary, six Muslim women from six different ethnic backgrounds are interviewed, who share their views regarding this traditional garment, as well as their thoughts on practicing Islam in the United States. Family members and husbands of these women are also interviewed to shed light on the spiritual and cultural dimensions of this practice. The video is accompanied by an instructor's manual (53 pages), which can be used for discussion in a classroom setting. Highly recommended.

95 *Young Voices from the Arab World: The Lives and Times of Five Teenagers*
Washington, D.C.: AMIDEAST, 1998. 30 min., col.
Grades 9–12
Each of the five teenagers from Egypt, Jordan, Kuwait, Lebanon, and Morocco takes the viewer of this video into their homes, schools, places of

worship and favorite entertainment spots, and shares particular aspects of Arab culture, language, religion, values and social customs. The video provides an opportunity for American and non-Muslim youths to learn from these young teenagers their views about families, education, the changing role of women, and hopes for the future. Historical, geographical, and other background information is also provided in this video. The film, which can be viewed in its entirety or in segments, can be adaptable for classroom use. It can be used along with the text with the same title (published in 1998). Included with the textbook is a teacher's guide that contains essays and statistics on the Arab world in general. Highly recommended for classroom use.

96 *Great World Religions: Islam*
Chantilly, Virginia: Teaching Co., 2003. 3 videodiscs (360 min.), col. +
    1 booklet (62 pp.)
ISBN: 156585649X
Grades 11–12

Created by John Esposito, one of the authorities on Islam, these two unique videodiscs cover twelve lectures or units for classroom teaching. Each of these units can be covered in thirty minutes. The contents of these units are: Lecture 1: Islam yesterday, today, and tomorrow; Lecture 2: The Five Pillars of Islam; Lecture 3: Muhammad, prophet and statesman; Lecture 4: God's word, the Qur'anic worldview; Lecture 5: The Muslim community, faith and politics; Lecture 6: Paths to God, Islamic law and mysticism; Lecture 7: Islamic revivalism, renewal and reform; Lecture 8: The contemporary resurgence of Islam; Lecture 9: Islam at the crossroads; Lecture 10: Women and change in Islam; Lecture 11: Islam in the West; Lecture 12: The future of Islam. These visual lessons cover all important aspects of Islam. The accompanying booklet should be very helpful as a guide. This set is a must for any high school class to learn about Islam. Highly recommended

HADITH

97 *Muslim Scouts Adventures*
Herndon, Virginia: Astrolabe Pictures, 1997. 78 min., col.
Grades K–5

This is a lively animated color video about a Muslim scout troop that travels to different countries solving mysteries, learning about Islamic history, and sight-seeing along the way. The places the scouts visit include Turkey, Burma, Zambia, Pakistan, and Egypt. The funny stories in this video reinforce positive morals and etiquette.

HISTORY AND POLITICS

98 *Ancient Civilizations: The Ottoman Empire*
Princeton, New Jersey: Films for the Humanities and Sciences, 1999.
47 minutes, col.
Grades 9–12
This film chronicles the majesty of the Ottoman Empire by examining its structure such as family, religion, and bureaucracy. Colorful illustrations, photographs, and maps reinforce the narrator's scholarly comments. The historical time period ranges from the sacking of Constantinople to the end of the sixteenth century. All of Eastern Europe, the Balkans, Algeria, Lebanon, Egypt, Spain, and Turkey were enveloped by the Ottomans. A fantastic resource for students and educators interested in this historical era. It is one of the thirteen-part series.

99 *Arab Americans*
Bala Cynwyd, Pennsylvania: Schlessinger Video Productions, 1993.
30 min., col.
ISBN: 1879151650
Grades 6–10
Part of the "Multicultural Peoples of North America Video Series," this documentary examines the heritage of different cultural groups. The Syrians, mostly Christians, immigrated to the United States in 1916 to seek their fortune. Many more Arabs, mostly Muslims from many Middle East countries, such as Lebanon, Jordan, Iraq, Egypt, Palestine, etc., moved to the United States in the 1960s either to seek refuge from their countries, or to look for better opportunities. The Zaher family from Jordan was one of the families of immigrants. Three generations of this family share memories of their country, and their motivation for journeying to the United States. The impact of Arab Americans on the growth of the United States, and the contributions made by individuals is also discussed. Very helpful source for those interested in learning the history of the first Arab immigrants to the United States, and the unique traditions they brought with them.

100 *Destruction* (Crusades, volume 4)
New York: British Broadcasting Corporation and A & E Home Video, 1995. 50 min., col.
ISBN: 1565015096
Grades 10–12
In this fourth and final series, presenter Terry Jones chronicles the unsuccessful Third and Fourth Crusades. By now crusading had very little to

do with religion. It was an institution. Richard "the Lionheart" and Philip
of France are added to the list of holy warriors. The narrator, Terry Jones,
examines the truth behind their noble deeds. The fourth and the final crusade was really a commercial operation. Constantinople was sacked and
looted by the crusaders. Revolts in Egypt destroyed the remnants of the
Crusaders' Christian kingdom. Highly recommended.

101 *Islam: Faith and Nations*
United States: MPI Home Video, 1983. 120 min. Color and black-and-
    white.
ISBN: 1556077726
Grades 6–12
Narrated by Sam Gray, the fascinating history of Islam from its beginnings 1300 years ago to the present is unfolded in this video. Islam is a mosaic composed of many nationalities from all over the world. Muhammad
founded Islam and told his followers that Allah was the one God and the
same one as in the Jewish and Christian religions. Since its founding, the
religion as well as its influence in science, mathematics, art, architecture,
etc. has spread throughout the world. This video is a marvelous treasure of
history.

102 *Jerusalem* (Crusades, volume 2)
New York: British Broadcasting Corporation and A & E Home Video,
    1995. 50 min., col.
ISBN: 156501507x
Grades 10–12
In the first volume of this series, the crusaders had reached the threshold
of Asia, but Jerusalem was still more than one thousand miles distant. Most
of the Christians and Muslims who had met en route never lived to see
Jerusalem. The presenter, Terry Jones, chronicles the crusaders' trail of car-
nage across the Middle East, following their path to Antioch, site of the
famed siege whose strange outcome would encourage the savagery of the
crusaders' campaign. In the conquest of Jerusalem, they sacked the city and
butchered the inhabitants.

103 *Jihad* (Crusades, volume 3)
New York: British Broadcasting Corporation and A & E Home Video,
    1995. 50 min., col.
ISBN: 1565015088
Grades 10–12

The third volume in the series (The Crusades) explains how eighty-eight years after the crusaders had conquered Jerusalem and had established a Christian Kingdom that extended as far as Egypt, the Muslims recaptured Jerusalem after uniting in a Holy War, Jihad. Nur ed-Din had declared himself a Prophet of God, and the leader of the Jihad, but he was not the leader who captured Jerusalem. Saladin was the leader who succeeded in defeating the crusaders. Highly recommended.

104 *Pilgrims in Arms* (Crusades, volume 1)
New York: British Broadcasting Corporation and A & E network, 1995.
    50 min., col.
ISBN: 1565015061
Grades 10–12
This first volume of the series (The Crusades) discusses how the crusaders, European Christians dedicated to taking Jerusalem from the infidels, and how Muslims, descended from all parts of Europe to liberate the Holy Lands. This documentary chronicles the origins of the crusades from Pope Urban II's hunger for military power to the successful propaganda of history's mass communication and recruitment campaigns. Even though the First Crusade was not successful, it set the stage for future crusades. Should appeal to teenagers because of humor used by host Terry Jones. Highly recommended.

HOLY DAYS

105 *Ramadan*
Bala Cynwyd, Pennsylvania: Schlessinger Video Productions, 1996. 25 min.,
    color, closed caption.
Grades K–3
An outstanding resource for children to learn about Ramadan, a month-long religious observance that begins on the ninth month of the Islamic calendar. Children will learn the story of Muhammad and the Qur'an, the meaning of the Five Pillars of Islam, and the importance of fasting, prayer, and sacrifice offered in honor of Allah. Highly recommended for school libraries.

106 *Ramadan: A Fast of Faith*
Princeton, New Jersey: Films for the Humanities & Sciences, 1999. 52 min.,
    col.
Grades 9–12

Ramadan or fasting, the Fourth Pillar of Islam, is the most sacred fast of the year. This program, beautifully filmed in Java and Sumatra, describes through the eyes of a young Muslim couple the rituals associated with Ramadan, the month-long Muslim fast, as practiced in Java and Sumatra; Id al-Fitr, the Muslim festival celebrated at the end of the Ramadan; sahur (the chanting of the Qur'an); and the Nights of Power are also explained.

107 *The Hajj: One American's Pilgrimage to Mecca, Friday, April 18, 1997*
United States: MPI Home Video, 2004. (ca. 22 min.), col.
ISBN: 1562789996
Grades 7–10
Since non-believers are forbidden to enter the sacred site of Mecca, this marvelous color video hosted by ABC News *Nightline*'s Ted Koppel, can be used to teach an understanding of one of the Five Pillars of Islamic faith—the Hajj. Hajj is an obligation to travel at least once in one's lifetime to the holiest city of Islamic religion, Mecca. Mecca is revered by all Muslims as the city of Abraham, the Prophet Muhammad, Haggar and her son Ishmad. An excellent resource.

INTERRELIGIOUS STUDIES

108 *Inside Islam*
New York: A & E Television Networks; distributed by New Video, 2002.
        102 min., col.
Grades 9–12
Originally aired on the History channel and produced by MPH Entertainment, Inc., this documentary is a crucial tool for educators, parents, etc. to develop an understanding of Islam and the relationship to Christianity and Judaism. It will facilitate lifting the veil of mystery surrounding what is often misunderstood about Islam. Absolutely enlightening.

109 *Islam and Christianity*
Princeton, New Jersey: Films for the Humanities & Sciences, 2003. 30 min.,
        col.
Grades 9–12
Iran's ambassador to the Vatican, Mohammad Masjed Jame'i, discusses the historical relations between Islam and Christianity. The basic differences and similarities between Islam and Christianity, the roles of Muhammad and Christ, the Qur'an and the Bible, and the long history of conflict

between them are examined as well. In addition, the reasons for the continuing conflict between Islam and the West are presented in this video. It is an excellent resource to promote understanding and tolerance between two major religions.

110 *The Wisdom of Faith*
Princeton, New Jersey: Newbridge Communications, 1996. 50 min., col.
Grades 9–12
In this interesting videocassette release of a television series originally broadcast on PBS, Bill Moyers interviews Huston Smith, an authority on the different religions of the world. Smith, who is a Methodist, and was introduced to Islam by the Sufis, relates his experiences that are similar to the traditions of Islam. For example, he prays five times a day as Muslims do. More appropriate for a high school college prep or an honors class.

111 *Towards Understanding Islam: A Perspective for Christians*
Harrisburg, Pennsylvania: Morehouse Publishing, 1992. 60 min., col.
Grades 9–12
The main purpose of this video is to explain the relationship between the two major religions of the world—Christianity and Islam. It describes Muhammad's revelations from Allah and the founding of Islam, its tenets, as well as the spread and history of Islam. The major contributions of the Islamic scholars are also explored. The Palestinian issue and its conflict with the Western world remain to be unresolved. Contains very useful information to eliminate stereotypes and promote understanding of the two religions.

ISLAMIC FAITH AND PRACTICE

112 *Hajj: The Pilgrimage*
Princeton, New Jersey: Films for the Humanities & Sciences, 1999. 53 min., col.
ISBN: 0736524274
Grades 9–12
Millions of Muslims travel to Mecca to participate in the sacred pilgrimage, the Hajj—the fifth pillar of faith. This documentary presents the day-by-day events of one such pilgrimage, which includes the ritual of tawaf (the circumambulation of the Ka'bah seven times), the performance of wuquf on Mount Rahman, the overnight stay at Muzdalifah, the symbolic stoning of the Devil in the valley of Mina, and the festival of sacrifice. It

also includes the changing of the embroidered cover on the Ka'bah, and the historical background on Islam and the Prophet Muhammad. A very interesting documentary for those who wish to learn about one of the Five Pillars of Islam—the Hajj.

113 *Living Islam: Foundations*
New York: Ambrose Video Publication, 1993. 50 min., col.
Grades 8–12

In association with BBC-TV, Ambrose Video Publishing produced this video to explain the tenets of faith essential to Islam. It demonstrates how Muslims use the Prophet Muhammad's life as an example to balance religion and life. An interesting segment is about a man in Mali converting villagers to Islam. Significant other religious sites around the world and people involved in the religion provide an insight into Muslim life in today's world.

114 *The Five Pillars of Islam*
Princeton, New Jersey: Films for the Humanities, 1983. 52 min. col.
Grades 9–12

Part of the series "The World of Islam," and narrated by Ian Holm, this documentary describes and puts into historical context the essential principles on which Islam rests—its five pillars. The Five Pillars of Islam are: the testimony of faith, prayer, giving zakat (support of the needy), fasting during the month of Ramadan, and the pilgrimage to Mecca once in a lifetime for those who are able. The program also introduces the international mosaic of Muslim believers, and the conflict between traditional teaching and the effects of industrialization.

115 *The Koran: The Holy Book of Islam*
Chicago: Britannica Films & Video, 1995. 14 min., col.
ISBN: 0782611079
Grades 6–12

This excellent video program traces the origins of the Qur'an, which is regarded by Muslims as the true word of God as revealed to the Prophet Muhammad. The documentary also discusses the five basic elements in Islam, known as "the Five Pillars of Islam," upon which the life of a religious Muslim is built. According to this program, the Qur'an has tremendous as well as sacred significance for Muslims, and it is the primary source of Islamic law regulating both religious and social life. A very interesting video that should appeal to Muslims as well as non-Muslims. Highly recommended for school libraries.

116 *The Message: The Story of Islam*
Troy, Michigan: Anchor Bay Entertainment, 1998. 2 videocassettes (228
    minutes), col.
Grades 11–12
    Produced and directed by Moustapha Akkad, and set in the seventh cen-
tury in Mecca, this documentary chronicles the history of Islam. It took six
years to prepare and one year to film this breathtaking large-scale documentary. Anthony Quinn and Irene Papas star in this video. Also includes
the documentary on the making of the film, titled "The Making of an epic."
Due to the length of these videos, they can be shown in shorter segments.

117 *The Secret Mecca*
Princeton, New Jersey: Films for the Humanities & Sciences, 2003. 54 min.,
    col.
Grades 10–12
    One of the five pillars of faith, the Hajj or the pilgrimage to Mecca, at-
tracts around three million worshipers to that holy site annually. In this documentary, the progress of a group of pilgrims privileged to follow in the
footsteps of God's prophet, Muhammad, is traced. The group, while spending fifteen days traveling together from Jedda, their entryway into Saudi
Arabia, to Medina, and Mecca, share their feelings, beliefs, and a strong
sense of bonding. This valuable source of firsthand information, which offers a behind-the-scenes visit to a sacred Muslim shrine not open to tourists,
also gives a thorough background on Muhammad.

118 *Understanding Islam and the American Muslim Community: A Visit to
    a Mosque in America*
Sterling, Virginia: Astrolabe Pictures, 2002. 58 minutes, col.
Grades 8–12
    Islam, the fastest growing religion in the United States is not well under-
stood by many Americans. This beautiful and interesting documentary takes
the viewer to the inside life of a Muslim community at the Islamic Center
of Greater Cincinnati. Visitors are guided through the buildings of the Center where various themes are presented: the Mosque is for worship and the
visitors are taught about the Five Pillars of Islam (faith, prayer, support of
the needy, fasting, pilgrimage to Mecca). The Community Center is used for
family and social recreation, the Academy is used for education, and the
Cultural Center is utilized for visitors to learn about Islam in America. A
few individuals who converted to Islam share their thoughts regarding their
new faith. The role of women in Islam is clarified, which is consistent with

the teachings of Islam. In addition, this documentary also presents dominant architectural and artistic features of the Islamic Center such as arches,
domes, minarets, and calligraphy. An excellent documentary.

MUSLIM CULTURE AND CUSTOMS

119 *Arabs, Muslims & Islam*
Auburn Hills, Michigan: Teacher's Discovery, 2002. 40 min., col.
Grades 6–12
   Who are Muslims? What is Islam? These are the two important questions
discussed in a four-country tour of Lebanon, South Africa, Malaysia, and
the United States. It is a very student-oriented video in that the people interviewed are teenagers talking about Islam. The program also discusses
the fact that regardless of the religion or geographic area, the interests of
this age group are alike. It is an excellent teacher's tool for introduction of
Islam to teenagers.

120 *Heart of the Koran*
Wheaton, Illinois: The Theosophical Society in America, 1990. 29 min.,
      col.
ISBN: 0815640000
Grades 9–12
   Lex Hixon, a North American Sufi Muslim, explores the Sufi Muslim
tradition of meditation and the Qur'an. The Holy Qur'an lies at the heart of
the practice and faith of Islam. A fascinating footage of a traditional Zikr
ceremony with costumed Sufi Dervishes from the Halveti-Jerrah Order and
the chanting passages from the Qur'an are featured. A wonderful educational tool for illustrating a different aspect of Islam.

121 *Hijab: An Act of faith*
Chicago: Sound Vision, 1998. 38 min., col.
Grades 8–12
   An excellent documentary regarding the hijab (head scarf) worn by Muslim women, and clarification of the misconceptions and stereotype impres-
sions by non-Muslims pertaining to the hijab. In this video, several very
highly educated Muslim women and converts from Canada and the United
States express their opinions and comments regarding the importance of
wearing hijab. They relate their personal experiences before and after they
started wearing hijab. Many Islamic women see their mode of dress as a

form of freedom from the unrelenting obsession with the female body. They believe that the priority is not how you appear to others on the outside, but who you are and how you affect others as a person, and that the negative baggage around hijab often results in a great deal of stress for Muslim women. Nikab, another form of covering of the face by some Muslim women, which was initially practiced by the wives of prophets, is also explained. Very highly recommended for any non-Muslim in order to get a clear understanding regarding the hijab.

122 *I Am a Sufi, I Am a Muslim*
Princeton, New Jersey: Films for the Humanities & Sciences, 1996. 52 min., col.

Grades 10–12

Originally broadcast in 1994 on Belgian Radio and Television, this program introduces Sufism, a branch of Islam which is less well known than some of the more fundamentalist forms in the West. The documentary is shot in India, Pakistan, Turkey, and Macedonia to find out exactly what Sufism is, and how it is observed in various parts of the world. Some of the features in the program are the whirling dervishes of Turkey, who find God through ecstasy, fakirs in Macedonia, and the very important role that music plays in Sufism in India and Pakistan. One of the most renowned performers of Qawali music, the late Nusrat Fateh Ali Khan, is also featured in this program. Quite intriguing.

123 *Islam with David McCullough*
Washington, D.C.: PBS Smithsonian World, 1987. 60 min., col.

Grades 8–12

This comprehensive video presents an extraordinary, picturesque explanation of Islam from its beginning to its increasing role in western contemporary society. Offers a very comprehensive in-depth explanation. Highly recommended; a five-star production.

124 *Islam: A Closer Look*
Chicago: Sound Vision, 1995. 29 min., col.

Grades 9–12

Very well documented, this video discusses several aspects of Islam, the world's fastest growing religion. Dr. Abdullah Hakim, an Islamic scholar; Hakeem Olajuwan, the basketball superstar; Hamza Yusuf, an American-born teacher and a student of Islam; and Nancy Ali, a former Roman Catholic nun and a convert to Islam, are among some of the individuals who share their views and comments regarding various subjects pertaining to Islam, such as the miracles of the Qur'an, Muslim family importance, equality between the genders including women's role in Islam, contributions of Muslims throughout the history and their impact on the way we live, and the importance of Islamic schools in the Islamic Centers. The last few minutes of the documentary are devoted to clarifying some of the stereotype misconceptions of Islam, and explaining the Five Pillars of Islam and their importance in a Muslim's life. Very interesting and highly recommended.

125 *Islam: There Is No God but God*
New York: Ambrose Video, 1993. 52 min., col.
Grades 9–12
This program, the fifth of the series titled "The Long Search" was a red ribbon winner at the American Film Festival. It exposes the viewer to Islam, a religion followed by 400 million people. The program, set in Egypt, depicts Sufi practice in a mosque, a children's free hospital, Egyptians returning from the Hajj travel, and a wedding at an oasis village. The discussions in regard to the beliefs and practices of the Islamic faith are very enlightening.

126 *Islamic Mysticism: The Sufi Way*
New York: Wellspring Media, 1997. 26 min, col.
ISBN: 1885538731
Grades 7–12
Huston Smith takes an in-depth look at various aspects of Sufism, a sect of Islam, that was formed to purify their practice of Islam. Often referred to as the "soul" of Islam, the video shows Sufi scenes in locations from India to Morocco with shots of breath-taking images of Muslim art and architecture and fascinating religious rituals. Extremely interesting.

127 *Mosque*
Maryknoll, New York: Maryknoll World Video, 1992. 28 min., 30 sec., col.
Grades 10–12
Hosted by Father Bill Grimm, filmed in Cairo, Egypt, this video provides non-Muslims with an introduction to Islam and to a mosque, a symbol of Islam. The inside and outside of a mosque are shown. Topics covered are: daily call of prayer, Five Pillars of Islam, the architecture and decoration of mosques, and the various steps followed before and during prayers in a mosque. Father Lance Nadeau, originally from the United States, who now

lives in Egypt, is also interviewed by Father Grimm for his views on Islam. Quite informative and interesting.

128 *Muslims*
New York: Mystic Fire Video, 2002. 117 min. col.
Grades 4–6
America's perception of Islam, the world's second largest religion, is dominated by misconceptions and lack of understanding. This documentary, which takes an in-depth look at what it means to be a Muslim in the twenty-first century, was filmed in Egypt, Malaysia, Iran, Turkey, Nigeria, and the United States. The influence of culture and politics on religion is explored. The film provides a deeper understanding of the political forces at work among Muslims around the world. In addition to exploring Islam's kinship with Christianity and Judaism, this film also looks at diverse interpretations of Islam among the Muslim people.

MUSLIMS IN THE WEST

129 *Choosing Islam*
Chicago: Sound Vision, 1993. 50 min., col.
Grades 10–12
Written, directed, and narrated by Gerard Earl Bilal, and presented by the Islam Circle of North America, this documentary introduces the doctrines of Islam, which include the Five Pillars of Islam. Some of the Americans, including the former pastor Rephael Naridaez, and the famous singer Yusuf Islam, present their views, observations, and the reasons they converted to Islam. The reasons as to why there is negativity associated with the Islam religion are also presented. Describes briefly the Nation of Islam and Malcolm X's observations of brotherhood practiced by Muslims of all colors and races, during his visit to Mecca for Hajj. Some Arabic captions of quotations from the Qur'an are included. A truly enlightening and educational video for understanding why people choose to convert to Islam.

130 *Islam Rising. The Qur'an and the American Dream*
Princeton, New Jersey: Films of the Humanities & Sciences, 2000. 52 min. col.
Grades 11–12
Consisting of eight million Muslims currently living in the United States, Islam has become a significant social force in America. Some Americans

fear the power of this growing religious group. This documentary traces the fast growth of Islam in New York City, and features commentary from the Council on American-Islamic Relations, which "strives to dispel prejudicial stereotypes and counter legal injustices." In this video, Reverend Jesse Jackson adds his voice of support for this religious group. Thought provoking and interesting.

131 *Muslims in America: Islam in Exile*
Princeton, New Jersey: Films for the Humanities & Sciences, 2003. 57 min. col.
ISBN: 0736586512
Grades 11–12
The surprisingly rapid growth of Islam in the heart of America's Bible Belt, a predominantly fundamentalist Christian locale, is examined in this program. The daily challenge for Muslims living in Appalachia is not so much in acceptance by their neighbors as with practicing their religion in a country whose overall culture is so often at odds with their own beliefs. Refugees living in the region and experts in American Islam are interviewed. Other highlights of this program are the history of Islam, Islamic contributions to the arts and sciences, and common ground between Muslims and Christians.

132 *Muslims in America: The Misunderstood Millions*
Orland Park, Illinois: MPI Home Video, 1997. 22 min., col.
ISBN: 1562789791
Grades 9–12
The immediate reaction by many individuals after the Oklahoma City bombing was to blame the Muslims. This program was originally broadcast on May 5, 1995, on the ABC television program entitled *Nightline* in which Ted Koppel's focus was to dispel stereotypes by introducing American Muslims from Cedar Rapids, Iowa, and examine the tenets of the Muslim faith. A valuable teaching tool to help promote diversity.

NATION OF ISLAM

133 *This Far by Faith: African-American Spiritual Journeys*
United States: Blackside, Inc., the Faith Project: distributed by PBS Video, 2003. 60 min. Black-and-white, and col.
Grades 8–12

A wonderful insightful view of the leaders and beliefs of The Nation of Islam. Elijah Muhammad was the first major leader, but his son Warith Deen transformed the religion to more closely follow the practice of orthodox Islam. After Elijah Muhammad's death, disagreement between Louis X Farrakhan and Warith Muhammad caused a split in the religion. Farrakhan in 1978 followed the old ideology, whereas Warith followed traditional Islam. This is Episode 5 from the series titled "Inheritors of the Faith."

RESISTANCE VERSUS TERRORISM

134 *An Intellectual Discourse: The Facts about Islam*
Brookings: South Dakota State University Instructional Technologies Center, 2001. 113 minutes, col.
Grades 11–12
Organized by the Office of Diversity Enhancement at the South Dakota State University, this forum on Islam is led by four professors from SDSU. In addition to discussing the history, beliefs, and practices of Islam, the panelists, in light of the events of September 11, 2001, examine the role of the news media in covering Islam and emphasize Islam's repudiation of terrorism. An interesting question-and-answer session follows the forum, however, it is rather difficult to understand the questions and answers due to a lack of clarity.

135 *Arab Americans after 9-11: Epilogue to Tales from Arab Detroit*
Los Angeles: Olive Branch Productions, 2003. 10 min., col.
Grades 10–12
Discusses how the Arab population of Detroit, Michigan, reacted to 9/11. The people interviewed expressed pride of their heritage, but indicated that they were equally proud of being Americans.

136 *Bin Laden: The Man Who Declared War on America*
Ashland, Oregon: Blackstone Audio-books, 2002. 18 sound discs (ca. 23 hours, 30 min.), col.
ISBN: 0786195363
Grades 10–12
Narration of these audio-discs is by the award-winning British narrator Nadia May. The author is an internationally renowned military and threat analyst. It is truly a comprehensive account of the rise of bin Laden, and the events in his life that turned him and those he leads into radical Islam's

terror network against the West. Highly informative and educational. Due to the length of the sound discs, it may be advisable to intersperse the segments.

137 *Brothers and Others: The Impact of September 11th on Arabs, Muslims, and Southeast Asians in America*
Seattle, Washington: Arab Film Distribution, 2002. 60 min. col.
Grades 9–12
   This is a documentary video about the "hidden" victims of 9/11, the thousands of Arabs and Muslims who have been detained without trial and many of those whose lives have been shattered. Some of the participants in the film are Muslim Chaplain Ms. Sanaa Nadim; author and professor Noam Chomsky; ACLU attorney Lucas Guttentag; and the executive director of the New York Council on American-Islamic Relations. The film follows a number of immigrants and Americans as they struggle in the heightened climate of hate, FBI investigations, and economic hardships that erupted as a result of the attacks on the World Trade Center and the Pentagon.

138 *Islam and War*
Princeton, New Jersey: Films for the Humanities & Sciences, 1994. 30 min. col.
ISBN: 0736573100
Grades 10–12
   Considered the spiritual head of the Hezbollah, and a leading political figure in the Lebanese Islamic Movement, Sayed Fadlallah presents his views of Jihad or Holy War, its rules, its origins, and the role of terror in such a war. The role of terror and violence in the contemporary world as seen by Muslim thinkers, and the reasons why some feel the need to wage a Holy War are also examined in this documentary, which is part of the series titled "Islamic Conversations." Fadlallah believes that acts of kidnapping, hijacking, use of bombs, and assassination of civilians for political reasons are wrong. According to Sayed Fadlallah, the Islamic resistance is not any different from resistance practiced by other cultures. It is an interesting documentary, particularly for those who wish to find out about Jihad and terrorism, yet from another perspective.

139 *Islam in America after September 11th*
Sterling, Virginia: produced by Vital Visuals; distributed by Astrolabe Islamic Media, 2002. 57 minutes. col.
Grades 10–12

Several American Muslims from around the United States through interviews share their stories and memories regarding the September 11 tragic attack. The impact of the 9/11 attack on the American Muslim community in the United States is also shared with the audience. In addition, American Muslims explain Islam to churches, various community groups and governments. Issues related to harassment of Muslims, and civil rights are also discussed.

140 *NOW with Bill Moyers: Facing East, Facing West*
Princeton, New Jersey: Films for the Humanities & Sciences, 2002. 4 video
cassettes (142 min.), col.
ISBN: 0736580808
Grades 11–12
This set consists of four volumes. v.1: Zaid Shakir on being Muslim in America—v.2: Azizah al-Hibri on interfaith dialogue—v.3: Karen Armstrong on religious fundamentalism—v.4: John Esposito on the struggles of Islam. As the title of this documentary indicates, the faithful of Islam face the East in prayer; however, some Muslims also face the West with a growing sense of worry and anger. In this four-part series, Bill Moyers discusses with leading experts on Islam some of the issues that are of concern to many individuals since 9/11.

141 *Terrorism: Aims and Objectives*
Princeton, New Jersey: Films for the Humanities & Sciences, 1995. 3
videocassettes (52 min. each), col.
Grades 9–12
The focus of this documentary is an attempt to describe the origins, growth, and effects of the following major groups in international terrorism: Abu Nidal, the Palestinians, and the Shite fundamentalists. Narrated by Julian Pettifer, this documentary is organized in three volumes titled: v.1: International Terrorism; v.2: Terror and Counter: Can Democracy Survive; v.3: Domestic Terrorism. The main focus of these videos is to explore the origins, growths, and effects of the major groups who are involved in international terrorism. The videos also show why highly motivated and intelligent terrorists are so difficult to catch, and the inevitable temptations for government to bend or break the law to bring the terrorists to justice. Due to the length of the videos, it may be necessary to watch them in segments, and follow with discussion. Highly recommended for high school students who wish to learn more about terrorism.

142 *The Islamic Wave*
Princeton, New Jersey: Films for the Humanities & Sciences, 2000. 50 min.,
    col.
Grades 11–12
   This program explores Islam, the world's second largest religion, by ex-
amining its increasing popularity and considering the use of violence by
Muslim extremists to achieve their goals. The sociopolitical landscape of
Islamic hotspots in the Middle East, Pakistan, Indonesia, and Sudan are ex-
amined as well.

143 *The Sword of Islam*
KCET Los Angeles PBS. 90 min., col.
Grades 9–12
   This video is highly recommended to gain an understanding of the rise of
Islamic Jihad in Egypt and Hezbollah in Lebanon. The producers use per-
sonal interviews as well as historical film footage. The goal of Hezbollah
and Islamic Jihad is to create an Islamic State or Republic similar to Iran.

WOMEN IN ISLAM

144 *Behind the Veil: Afghan Women under Fundamentalism*
Princeton, New Jersey: Films for the Humanities & Sciences, 2003. 26
    min., col.
ISBN: 0736538852
Grades 11–12
   For women who lived in Afghanistan under repressive Taliban rule, beat-
ings, rape, and enslavement took place commonly. This film, made during
the Taliban's regime, discusses the massive human rights abuses that have
been escalating since the withdrawal of the Soviet forces from Afghanistan,
as seen through the eyes of women who have survived years of gender and
religious intolerance. Women's groups fought for freedom and democracy,
and their resistance activities carried out are also documented in this film.
Some of the content of this film may be objectionable due to the violence.

145 *Benaat Chicago: Growing Up Arab and Female in Chicago*
Chicago: Chicago Center of the American Friends Service Committee,
    1996. 30 min.
Grades 10–12

This documentary was produced after a year-long collaboration of the directors—Jennifer Bing-Canar and Mary Zerkel, with Arab-American teenagers to document their lives while growing up on the southwest side of Chicago. In addition to addressing stereotypes and racism towards Arabs and Arab women, this video also highlights what makes many Arab Americans proud of their cultural heritage. It is a thought-provoking and insightful documentary, particularly for those who wish to learn more about women in Islam.

146 *Death by Stoning: Justice, Punishment, and Human Rights*
Princeton, New Jersey: Films for the Humanities & Sciences, 2003. 23 min.
(color)
ISBN: 0736582754
Grades 9–12
Under Islamic law (Sharia), the bearing of a child out of wedlock is a capital offense, for which the punishment is death by stoning. Produced by ABC News, this program, set in Nigeria, is about the case of a young woman, Amina Lawal, who was sentenced to death by an all-male jury. Her situation and the concepts of justice and punishment in relation to human rights is the main topic of discussion. Akbar Ahmed, American University, and Ayesha Imam, who assisted in Ms. Lawal's defense, are the principal discussants.

147 *Islam, the Veil and the Future*
Alexandria, Virginia: PBS Video, 1980. 30 min., col.
ISBN: 0559512628
Grades 10–12
An interview with Nuha Alegelan, wife of the Saudi Arabian ambassador to the United States, highlights the misconception regarding the role of women in Islamic society. Although this program was filmed in the 1980s, many of the responses in the documentary hold true today. Participants' questions and comments are discussed as well.

5

Fiction and Folklore

One will find listed in this chapter thirty-six resources regarding novels, short stories, children's stories, picture books, and famous Arabic folktale translations. Out of these thirty-six resources, one is for high school, eight are for middle school, and twenty-seven are for elementary school grade levels.

148 *The Farmer's Wife*
Cambridge, Massachusetts: Hoopoe Books, 1998. [34] pp.
ISBN: 1883536073
Grades K–5
   This is one of the many Sufi teaching tales of a farmer's wife who is trying to retrieve an apple from a hole in the ground. She seeks help from a bird and a cat, but to no avail. Finally, it is the wind that blows off the apple from the hole. Supplemented by striking color illustrations.

149 *Attar: Stories for Young Adults*
Attar, Farid al-Din; Muhammad Nur Abdus Salam; illustrated by Rose Ghajar Bakhtiar.
ABC International Group; Chicago: distributed by KAZI Publications, 2000. 202 pp.
ISBN: 1930637055; ISBN (pbk.): 1930637063
Grades 7–12
   Translated and adapted from the Persian, this series of stories for young adults is to encourage young adults to turn to an important literary heritage. Although these stories could be read to younger children, they are more appropriate for older children. The stories are adapted from the writings of Farid al-Din Attar, one of the giants of Islamic, Persian, and

world literature around 1136 C.E. They are translated and adapted from the Persian by Muhammad Nur Abdus Salam. Includes illustrations.

150 *A Prince of Islam*
Barker, Carol.
Reading, Massachusetts: Addison-Wesley, 1977. 35 pp.
ISBN: 0201004240
Grades 3–4
The author presents a fictional story of a young prince whose father is Caliph of the Muslim Empire during the ninth century. The simple text and illustrations describe the young prince's childhood. A good book for young readers.

151 *Samir and Yonatan*
Carmi, Daniella; translated by Yael Lotan.
New York: Arthur A. Levine Books, 2000. 183 pp.
ISBN: 0439135044. ISBN: (pbk.) 0439135230
Grades 4–6
Samir, a Palestinian boy, is sent to an Israeli hospital for surgery. He is surrounded by the very people he blames for his brother's death. While in the hospital, he begins to learn about the Israeli kids around him. He discovers their hurts and conflicts, and shares his own. He develops a friendship with an Israeli boy, Yonatan. This is a story of violence and healing — the story of a boy facing the enemy he has been taught to fear. This book was honored with the prestigious Mildred Batchelder Award, given by the American Library Association for the most distinguished work of translated literature each year. Includes a glossary. "Daniella Carmi's story provides insight into many aspects of the Israeli/Palestinian conflict and points to children as the hope for resolution." — a reviewer. "A Palestinian boy comes to terms with his younger brother's death by an Israeli soldier in this slow-paced but affecting novel originally published in Hebrew in 1994." — *Publishers Weekly*

152 *A Stone in my Hand*
Clinton, Cathryn.
Cambridge, Massachusetts: Candlewick Press, 2002. 191 pp.
ISBN: 0763613886
Grades 5–8
Set in a Palestinian community in Gaza City during 1988 and 1989, this story is about Malaak, an eleven-year-old girl whose father disappears

while looking for work in Israel. Tensions grow between Palestinians and Israelis. Malaak gets very concerned when she finds out that her brother Hamid and his friend Tariq had become involved with a group of young radicals, and feared that they may be the next victims of hate. This is a story that reminds readers that children in the Middle East live with the threat of terrorism and war. Includes a glossary of Arabic words and their English meanings. "Clinton has created a rich, colorful cast of characters and created an emotionally charged novel." — *School Library Journal*

153 *Seven Daughters & Seven Sons*
Cohen, Barbara and Bahija Lovejoy.
New York: Beech Tree Books, 1994. 220 pp.
ISBN: 0688135633
Grades 10–12
 In this romantic novel based on an Arabic folktale that has been a part of the oral tradition of Iraq since the eleventh century, one woman, named Buran, dares to be different. Buran refuses to sit at home and wait to be married to the man her father chooses. She is determined to earn a fortune by using her skills. She disguises herself as a boy, and travels to another city where she starts a successful business. The city's crown prince visits her shop, and soon Buran finds herself falling in love with this prince. She worries that if she reveals to the prince her true gender identity, she may lose everything she has worked for.

154 *Storia di Iqbal*
D'Adamo, Francesco; translated by Ann Leonori.
Waterville, Maine: Thorndike Press, 2004. 149 pp.
ISBN: 0786263857
Grades 4–6
 In many countries, bonded child labor is considered an indispensable part of the economic system. First published in Italian in 2001, this is a fictionalized account of a very courageous Pakistani child named Iqbal Masih, who worked in a carpet factory, but managed to escape from "forced and bonded labor." Iqbal Masih went to help free other young children like him from bonded labor before he got gunned down at the age of thirteen. It is a well-written and inspirational book, using large type, and is narrated by a young girl Fatima, whose life was forever changed by Iqbal's courage.

155 *The Legend of the Persian Carpet*
DePaola, Tomie; illustrated by Claire Ewart.

New York: G. P. Putnam's Sons, 1993. (unpaged)
ISBN: 0399224157
Grades K–3

It is a charming, beautifully illustrated children's folk-tale about the King's diamond that was stolen and shattered during the robbery. The light of the diamond became the inspiration for the pattern of the first Persian carpet. An inspiring story for young children. Includes color illustrations.

156 *Ahmed and the Nest of Sand: A Piping Plover Story*
Domm, Kristin Bieber; illustrated by Jeffrey C. Domm.
Halifax, Nova Scotia: Nimbus Publishing, 2000. 32 pp.
ISBN: 1551093383
Grades 3–5

This is a cumulative Sufi teaching tale of a farmer's wife who is trying to retrieve an apple from a hole in the ground. The text is complemented by color illustrations.

157 *Parvana's Journey*
Ellis, Deborah.
Toronto: Groundwood Books, 2002. 199 pp.
ISBN: 0888995148; ISBN (pbk.): 0888995199
Grades 5–8

A poignant sequel to *The Breadwinner*, Parvana is now a thirteen-year-old Afghan girl who is searching for her mother and siblings after the death of her father. Her journey entails constant vigilance to avoid Taliban soldiers, bombs, and landmines. Along the way, she encounters a young girl and a boy who become her traveling companions. Together they battle starvation, bombings, and despair before they reach a camp that offers hope. A black-and-white map is included. "Although American readers are half a world away, they will be moved by the tremendous suffering of the young characters who speak, think, and bicker like children everywhere." —*Booklist*

158 *The Breadwinner*
Ellis, Deborah.
Toronto: Douglas & McIntyre, 2001. 170 pp.
ISBN: 0888994192; ISBN (pbk.): 0888994168
Grades 5–8

A heart-wrenching fictional story of an eleven-year-old Afghan girl who disguised herself as a boy so she could earn money to support her family. Her father had been imprisoned by the Taliban. Due to the strict limitations imposed on females by the Afghan Taliban, she was the only one in the family, disguised as a boy, who could mingle freely in the streets of Kabul. Truly inspirational story for young girls. "The topical issues introduced, coupled with this strong heroine, will make this novel of interest to many conscientious teens." — *Publishers Weekly*

159 *Ali and the Spider*
El-Magazy, Rowaa; illustrated by Stevan Stratford.
Leicester, England: Islamic Foundation, 2000. 17 pp.
ISBN: 0860373258
Grades K–5

A beautifully colored, illustrated book written to perpetuate the folk story about the spider web that protects the followers of Muhammad from their enemies.

160 *Kids are Muslims Too: A Collection of Muslim Short Stories and Poetry for Children*
Ghandchi, Melody; illustrations by Siddiqa Juma.
Bethesda, Maryland: Islamic Education Center, 1990. 94 pp.
ISBN: 1871031370
Grades 4–6

Contains fifteen short, interesting stories and poetry for Muslim children. Each story includes illustrations in pastel colors, and has a moral. It is one of the books from the series "Series of Stories of Muslim Children." An excellent read-aloud book for young children.

161 *Grandfather's Orchard*
Ghazi, Abidullah; illustrated by Michele van Patten.
Chicago: IQRA International Educational Foundation, 1993. [18] pp.
ISBN: 1563163071
Grades K–5

This heartwarming story is about Ahmad, Asma, and their grandfather Abdullah. The children are anxious to help their grandfather who wants to plant an orchard of fruit trees. The highly regarded family tradition of planting the seeds for future generations among the Muslims is emphasized. The story may have to be read to younger children. Includes black-and-white illustrations.

162 *The Glory of Martyrdom*
Grougan, Hamid.

Tehran, Iran: Islamic Propagation Organization, 1983. 32 pp.
Grades 4–6

This is a story about Amr, a convert to the Islamic faith, who wishes to become a martyr defending Islam alongside the Holy Leader of Islam. Since he was lame, his family and friends did not want him to go into the battle to defend Medina. The Prophet gave Amr permission to fight in order to protect the city. Amr died in the battle fulfilling his wish never to return to Medina. Thus he became a martyr for his faith. A very inspirational story.

163 *Children's Stories Project*
Hutchinson, Uthman. Illustrated by Abdulmuttalib Fahema.
Beltsville, Maryland: Amana Publications, 1995. 6 books.
Grades 1–6

The Children's Story Project is a collection of thirty-six illustrated short stories, each book containing six stories, grouped by reading level, from grades one through six (ages six to eleven) of the American school system. The series centers on an American Muslim family living in a small American city. The parents, their three school-aged children, and their friends and relatives from America, Afghanistan, Pakistan, and Malaysia form the characters of the series. Aimed at providing a true picture of Muslim practice and culture as they exist in a contemporary setting, these delightful and entertaining stories are written about children for children of ages six to eleven. This series will be of great value to parents, children, and teachers. The titles are: *Crocodiles Pray* (Grade 1); *Jamaal's Jam* (Grade 2); *Muffins* (Grade 3); *Chicken Pox* (Grade 4); *In Anger* (Grade 5); and *The New Kid* (Grade 6).

164 *A Gift of Friendship*
Imtiaz, Razana; illustrations by Lubna Hoque.
Leicester, England: Islamic Foundation, 1997. 28 pp.
ISBN: 0860372642
Grades K–5

A profoundly moving story of a child who demonstrates universal values of compassion, courage, and sacrifice by giving her best toy to a child who does not have any. In the end, the child is rewarded with an unexpected beautiful new toy. The story may have to be read to younger children. Includes color illustrations.

165 *The Island of Animals: Adapted from an Arabic Fable*
Johnson-Davies, Denys; illustrated by Sabiha Khemir.

Austin, Texas: University of Texas Press, 1994. 76 pp.
ISBN: 0292740352; ISBN (pbk.): 0292740360
Grades 5–6

Adapted from the original book that was written in Arabic in the fourth century of the Islamic era (tenth century AD), this book expresses in the form of a fable the teachings of Islam about man's responsibilities toward animals. An inspiring story, accompanied by black-and-white illustrations, discusses how Allah created humans to be superior to other living creatures; however, Man has the responsibility to be accountable to judgment upon death as to how he lived his life, whereas other creatures do not. "An important book that will be enjoyed by adults and children alike, and a reminder to all of the importance of humane treatment of animals."
—*Publishers Weekly*

166 *Stories from the Muslim World*
Khattab, Huda; illustrated by M. Ishaq.
London: Ta-Ha Publishers, 1996. 44 pp.
ISBN: 1897940343
Grades 4–5

There are thirteen short stories about the beginnings of Islam, famous Muslim figures in history, and Muslim traditions and beliefs. These are interesting and easy-to-read stories handed down from generation to generation. Includes color illustrations. An excellent book for reluctant readers.

167 *My Name was Hussein*
Kyuchukov, Hristo; illustrated by Allan Eitzen.
Honesdale, Pennsylvania: Boyds Mills Press, 2004. 1 v. (unpaged)
ISBN: 1563979640
Grades 1–3

A heart-wrenching story set in Bulgaria of a young child who is affected by racial and religious prejudice. Young Hussein from a Muslim, Gypsy family lived in a small Bulgarian village. After World War II, the communist government persecuted minorities. In the mid 1980s, the government forced people who were not ethnic Bulgarians to change their names. Written from a child's perspective, this book demonstrates the personal price that one pays due to political oppression. Includes illustrations.

168 *The Flame Tree*
Lewis, Richard.
New York: Simon & Schuster Books for Young Readers, 2004. 276 pp.

ISBN: 0689863330
Grades 5–9

This is an interesting story about a twelve-year-old son of an American missionary doctor, living in Indonesia, who finds out a great deal about himself and Islam during the time he gets caught up in the middle of an international crisis. The story is set against the backdrop of September 11, 2001. It is a novel that promotes friendship, faith, and forgiveness. Questions about cultural and religious differences are addressed by the author in a creative way.

169 *The Desert Chief: Story of Thumama ibn Uthal*
Murad, Khurram.
Leicester, England: The Islamic Foundation, 1984. 24 pp.
ISBN: 0860371360; ISBN (pbk.): 0860371360
Grades 6–9

Exceptionally well-written, this wonderful story is about relationships. A powerful tribal chief, Thumama ibn Uthal, had set out to kill the Prophet Muhammad. However, after his capture, as a result of the humane and dignified treatment by the Prophet and his companions, the desert chief Thumama ibn Uthal converted to Islam. Color designs and illustrations complement the text.

170 *The Kingdom of Justice*
Murad, Khurram.
Leicester, England: The Islamic Foundation, 1983. 46 pp.
ISBN: 0860371230
Grades 5–9

Beautiful designs and color illustrations complement stories from the life of Umar. These stories recapture the rules of justice and equality before the law that pervaded the life of the first Islamic community. A wonderful book to inspire eleven- to fourteen-year-olds. It relates not only to the example of the Prophet Muhammad, but also to the six episodes from the life of the second Caliph, Umar bin al-Khattab. Includes texts on the Qur'an, the Sunnah, and other teachings of Islam.

171 *The Wise Poet: Story of Al-Tufayl Bin' Amr*
Murad, Khurram; illustrations by Hanife Hasan.
Leicester, England: Islamic Foundation, 1985. 23 pp.
ISBN: 0860371506
Grades 5–8

This is a story of Al-Tufayl Bin Amr, a respected chief of a tribe called Daws, who was known for reciting poems. On one of his visits to the Ka'bah, where poems were recited, he was very impressed by the prayer of a Muslim who was none other than the Blessed Prophet. Includes colored illustrations.

172 *Habibi*
Nye, Naomi Shihab.
New York: Simon & Schuster Books for Young Readers, 1997. 259 pp.
ISBN: 0689801491
Grades 5–9

This is a novel written by a distinguished anthologist and poet. When Liyana's father, a doctor and a native Palestinian moves his contemporary Arab-American family from St. Louis to Jerusalem, the fourteen-year-old Liyana's world shifts. The family, particularly Liyana, faces many cultural challenges and change. They must also deal with the tensions between Jews and Palestinians. A very interesting novel.

173 *The Space between Our Footsteps: Poems and Paintings from the Middle East*
Nye, Naomi Shihab.
New York: Simon & Schuster Books for Young Readers, 19998. 144 pp.
ISBN: 0689812337
Grades 7–12

The poems and paintings of more than one hundred writers and artists from nineteen countries are compiled by Naomi Shihab Nye in this book. The writers are from various countries within the Middle East. The poems are translated from their original languages, and therefore the reader will not have the benefit of the natural rhythms of the languages the poems were taken from. Several of the poems deal with loss, such as loss of loved ones, the loss of time, the loss of relationships, and the loss of basic human rights. Thirty-nine paintings, done in a rich assortment of styles and mediums, from figurative to folk art, abstract to collage, are included in this book. This collection can be of interest to all who are interested in this subject, including adults. Includes a comprehensive introduction, a map, and short biographies of the contributors. "Nye's respect and admiration for Middle Eastern culture and for poetry come through in the expertly chosen, artistically arranged entries."—*School Library Journal*

174 *The Hundredth Name*
Oppenheim, Shulamith Levey; illustrated by Michael Hays.

Honesdale, Pennsylvania: Boyds Mills Press, 1995. [28 pp.]
ISBN: 1563971836
Grades 3–5

This rich and eloquent story is about Saleh, whose simple faith and love for an animal is set in Muslim Egypt. Humans know ninety-nine names for Allah, but the hundredth name is a secret. Salah is sad because his camel is sad. Salah's father advises Salah to pray Allah for help, which he does. The next day, Salah notices that his camel does not appear to be sad, and Salah believes that this must be so because the camel must have now known the hundredth name of Allah. This story emphasizes the power of Muslim faith and daily power. Includes beautiful color acrylic-on-linen illustrations.

175 *The King, the Boy and the Sorcerer*
Salim, Umar and Salimah Salim.
Birmingham, England: Al-Hidaayah Publishing and Distribution, 1997. 33 pp.
ISBN: 1898649227
Grades 1–2

Beautifully illustrated, this touching story told by the Prophet is an interesting one that will help children appreciate and understand the importance of belief in Allah, in spite of trials.

176 *The Silly Chicken*
Shah, Idries.
Cambridge, Massachusetts: Hoopoe Books, 2000. [16] pp.
ISBN: 1883536197
Grades K–3

This charming and humorous book from an award-winning series of children's stories by Shah is about a chicken who learns to speak like humans. The chicken's warning causes the townspeople to panic. It teaches children not to be too gullible, and to think for themselves. It is one of the stories collected from the oral and written Sufi sources in Central Asia and the Middle East about one thousand years ago. Includes colored illustrations.

177 *The Lion Who Saw Himself in the Water*
Shah, Idries; illustrated by Ingrid Rodriguez.
Cambridge, Massachusetts: Hoopoe Books, 2003. [34] pages.
ISBN: 1883536316
Grades 1–2

This is a tale about a terrified lion that gets extremely thirsty as he growls at his own reflection in a pool of water that is shiny as a mirror. This story, originally told by the thirteenth-century Sufi poet Jalaluddin Rumi, is educational in that it teaches children to overcome irrational fears, often caused by behavior or circumstances that they as yet may not understand. The text is in English with Spanish translation, and is complemented by beautiful illustrations. "Brightly colored, cheerful illustrations express upbeat peaceful messages." — *Booklist*

178 *Neem the Half-Boy*
Shah, Idries; illustrated by Midori Mori & Robert Revels.
Cambridge, Massachusetts: Hoopoe Books, 1998. [16] pp.
ISBN: 1883536103
Grades K–3
   A moving story over a thousand years old, passed down by the Sufi tradition. The Queen of Hich-Hich gives birth to a half-boy because she did not faithfully follow the directions of Arif, the wise man. The heart of the story is regarding the half-boy's effort to become whole by confronting a dragon. Accompanied by beautiful color illustrations.

179 *The Magic Horse*
Shah, Idries; illustrated by Julie Freeman.
Cambridge, Massachuttes: Hoopoe Books, 1998. 34 pp.
ISBN: 1883536111; ISBN (pbk.): 188353626x
Grades 3–7
   This is a retelling of an ancient Sufi teaching tale set in the Middle East, in which two very different princes find their hearts' desires: one finds it in a wondrous mechanical fish, and the other one finds it in a magical wooden horse. Beautiful color illustrations by Julie Freeman capture the magic of this folktale. "Since little material from Sufi tradition is available for children, this book will be a welcome addition to traditional literature collections." — *School Library Journal*

180 *Haveli*
Staples, Suzanne Fisher.
New York: Random House, 1995, 320 pp.
Grades 8–12
   In this great sequel to "Shabanu: Daughter of the Wind," Shabanu, the youngest of Rahim's four wives, and her young daughter Mumtaz, are treated cruelly by Rahim's three older wives. The story takes place in Chollstan Desert of Pakistan. Shabanu flees to the *haveli*, Rahim's old family home in the city. She falls in love with a man whose life is ruled by the

very traditions that make the union impossible. Eventually, Shabanu must thread her way between conflicting loyalties to her husband and her family, and a path for herself and her daughter. Highly recommended for young adult readers. "A taut, suspenseful narrative with strong female characters and a terrific sense of place." — *The Horn Book*. "This engrossing novel will keep readers hooked." — *School Library Journal*

181 *Shabanu: Daughter of the Wind*
Staples, Suzanne Fisher.
New York: Alfred A. Knopf, Inc., 1991. 240 pp.
ISBN: 0679810307
Grades 8–12

An eleven-year-old Shabanu, the second daughter in a family with no sons, and whose home is the windswept Chollstan Desert of Pakistan, has been allowed freedom by her parents, which is forbidden to most Muslim girls. Her parents, who grow concerned that her independence will lead to trouble, arrange for her to marry an older man whose wealth will bring prestige to the family. Although this will mean an end to Shabanu's liberty, she accepts her father's wish as her duty to her family. In addition, due to the failure of her older sister's marriage plans, Shabanu is called upon to sacrifice everything she has dreamed of. Includes a list of "Names of characters," including their pronunciations, which are very helpful to the reader. It is a "Newbery Honor" and an "American Library Association Notable" book. "Exciting, well-written fantasy." — *Publisher's Weekly*. "A mesmerizing story . . . rich in detail, high in excitement, and filled with unforgettable characters." — *Booklist*

182 *A Boy from Makkah*
Yamani, Muhammad Abduh.
Chicago: IQRA International Education Foundation, 2002. 150 pp.
ISBN: 1563160579
Grades 3–6

Muhammad Abduh Yamani, one of Saudi Arabia's leading thinkers and humanists, writes this very interesting and inspirational fictional biography of a young boy. This young boy was deprived of opportunities; however, due to his faith, patience, and perseverance, succeeded in his life. This story reveals certain universal truths, primarily that caring for others and cooperating with others are very critical for both individual and community life.

183 *I Want to Talk to God*
Z'eghidour, Slimane; illustrated by Dominique Thibault; translated by
Sarah Mathews.
Mankato, Minnesota: Creative Education, 1997. 38 pp.
ISBN: 0886828244
Grades 3–6
Originally written in French, this is a moving story of a poor pious peasant who seeks God to find out why God had destined him to have the life he led, and why others were richer than he was. In the end the peasant, after traveling to many strange places and meeting many other people, meets God in the desert. The peasant learns that the greatest of all riches and rarest of all gifts is to accept what one is. Includes color illustrations.

6

General Reference Resources

In this chapter, a reader will find forty-one resources for traditional reference materials such as atlases, dictionaries, encyclopedias, almanacs, and additional resources relevant for research. These resources offer extended information about various subjects pertaining to Islam. Entries in this chapter are as follows: twenty-four for general readers, four for high school, four for middle school, and nine for elementary school grade levels.

ALMANACS

184 *The Muslim Almanac: A Reference Work on the History, Faith, Culture, and Peoples of Islam*
Nanji, Azim.
Detroit, Michigan: Gale Research, 1996. 581 pp.
ISBN: 081038924x
General Readers
   Well organized and contributed by thirty-six writers, each specialized in the subject they have contributed, this almanac provides a perspective on the historical formations of the worldwide Muslim community from Arabia to the Philippines. The writers' insights are based on research and on personal experiences from having lived in different parts of the Muslim world. The study of each region provides an interconnected setting for an overview of the cultural as well as intellectual accomplishments in Islamic contexts, including law, philosophy, science, theology, the arts and literature, education, and architecture. A lengthy bibliography at the end of the volume is followed by a detailed index, which can be used to

find any specific information. Includes color illustrations, and maps, and an index. Highly recommended for researchers.

ATLASES

185 *Historical Atlas of the Middle East*
Freeman-Grenville, G.S.P.
New York: Simon & Schuster, 1993. 144 pp.
ISBN: 0133909158
General Readers
   Containing 115 two-color collection of maps and informative text, this atlas gives an overview of the Middle East from 2500 B.C.E. to the present. A table of contents provides an easy access to the maps. A valuable resource for anyone interested in this region of the world. If the maps were in different colors instead of only two colors, this atlas would have been more effective and impressive. ". . . [W]ill be welcomed by staff and users in academic and large public libraries. Though there are several other atlases of the contemporary Middle East, this one is unique for its historical approach." — *Booklist*

186 *A Historical Atlas of Pakistan*
Greenberger, Robert.
New York: Rosen Pub. Group, 2003. 64 pp.
ISBN: 0823938662
Grades 5–8
   A thoroughly enlightening view of the political history of the people, and their religions, that influenced early Pakistan until the modern era. Includes bibliographical references, glossary, and index. Remarkable, interesting and an easy-to-read book. Includes some color maps and illustrations.

187 *Atlas of the Middle East*
Mehler, Carl.
Washington, D.C.: National Geographical Society, 2003. 96 pp.
ISBN: 0792250664
General Readers
   Iraq and surrounding countries in the Middle East raise curiosity worldwide due to tensions in those regions. This valuable atlas provides an indepth look at the forces responsible for acts of violence and costly wars in this region. It is a fascinating and excellent atlas containing newly re-

searched and the most current maps illustrating the various issues of the region. Visual explanations address questions surrounding religion, oil, agriculture, industry, ethnic groups, trade, international corporations, and military forces. In addition, the history of the Middle East is explained using maps devoted to the rise and fall of empires, civilizations, major conflicts, holy sites, and other important events that have impacted the region. Color maps and illustrations enhance the text. Highly recommended for all school libraries. "Geographically, politically, thematically, and chronologically organized, *National Geographic Atlas of the Middle East* is an accessible reference to a turbulent era prominent in headlines, heart, and minds." —*Editorial Review*

188 *Historical Atlas of the Islamic World*
Nicolle, David.
New York: Checkmark Books, 2003. 189 pp.
ISBN: 0816053324
General Readers
   The focus of this atlas is Islamic history from the time of the Prophet Muhammad until the start of the sixteenth century. The religion, culture, civilization, and arts of Islam, rich and fascinating in their own right, and less understood by not only non-Muslims but many Muslims as well, are included in this outstanding resource. The current interest in Islam justifies the timely publication of this atlas. The beautiful color photographs complement the text. Includes a list of books in European and Turkish languages for further reading, a list of museums in various countries of the world, and an index. An excellent resource for any public and senior high school library.

189 *A Historical Atlas of Iran*
Ramen, Fred.
New York: Rosen Publishing Group, 2003. 64 pp.
ISBN: 0823938646
Grades 5–8
   An outstanding resource about Iran containing dozens of color maps and photographs. The maps and text chronicle the history of this Middle Eastern country, formerly known as Persia. Topics such as ancient Iran, Second Persian Empire, coming of Islam, Mongol invasions, Third Persian Empire, Shahs, and independent Iran, qualify this book as an excellent reference book for any library. Includes a timeline, a glossary, and an index.

190 *A Historical Atlas of the United Arab Emirates*
Romano, Amy.
New York: Rosen Publishing Group, 2004. 64 pp.
ISBN: 0823945014
Grades 5–8

This atlas chronicles a fascinating history of the United Arab Emirates, a federation of seven independent sheikhdoms situated on the Arabian Peninsula. Its inhabitants are thought to be the first civilization to domesticate a camel. The geographical location of this area has created a contingent government over the ages. One of the newer governments in the world, the UAE was created in 1971. Historically influenced by the Greeks, the Persians, the Islamic nations, and the Europeans, it is a critical area of the Middle East. Includes a timeline, color maps and photographs, a glossary, and an index.

191 *A Historical Atlas of Yemen*
Romano, Amy.
New York: Rosen Publishing Group, 2004. 64 pp.
ISBN: 0823945022; ISBN (pbk.): 0823945014
Grades 3–7

The history of Yemen, one of the oldest inhabited regions of the world, yet one of the least known Arab nations, is chronicled in this atlas. During the ancient times, the country gained prominence for its trade in frankincense and myrrh; later on, it was famous for coffee, and currently for oil. Reputed to be the home of the Queen of Sheba, its geographic location has been a dominant part of history. Even today, its borders are disputed by neighboring countries. The atlas is enhanced by color maps and photographs, a timeline, a glossary, and an index. Highly recommended for libraries.

192 *A Historical Atlas of Saudi Arabia*
Stair, Nancy L.
New York: Rosen Publishing Group Inc., 2003. 64 pp.
ISBN: 0823938670; ISBN (pbk.): 0823938611
Grades 5–8

Using color maps and pictures, this beautifully organized atlas chronicles the history of Saudi Arabia—the country that leads the world in oil production. Topics covered in this book are the ancient Arabia, early tribes, power struggles, rise of Islam, Arabia after Muhammad, and the modern Saudi Arabia. Includes an index, timeline, a glossary, and a bibliography for "further reading." Well recommended.

DICTIONARIES AND ENCYCLOPEDIAS

193 *The A to Z of Islam*
Adamec, Ludwig W.
Lanham, Maryland: Scarecrow Press, 2002. 298 pp.
ISBN: 0810845059
General Readers
   This concise dictionary provides the serious student as well as the lay person a handy reference to acquire information on the Islamic religion and the culture. It includes short biographies of theologians, philosophers, founders of Sunni and Shi'ite schools of jurisprudence, and individuals who were a great influence on Islamic politics and culture from early days to the present. It also contains a list of abbreviations and acronyms, a chronology listing important dates from the sixth to the end of the twentieth century, and a comprehensive bibliography for further research. Well-organized resource for any library collection.

194 *Historical Dictionary of Islam*
Adamec, Ludwig W.
Lanham, Maryland: Scarecrow Press, 2001. 417 pp.
ISBN: 0810839628
Grades 9–12
   Written by Adamec, a known authority on Afghanistan, this is an essential reference dictionary that provides information on crucial Islamic people, basic concepts and practices, and significant stages and expansion of Islam. Includes a very useful introduction, chronology, and a bibliography. Includes a map. "This book is a good acquisition for most public libraries and a useful supplementary quick reference for academic libraries."
— *School Library*

195 *The Children's Encyclopaedia of Arabia*
Beardwood, Mary.
London: Stacey International, 2001. 160 pp.
ISBN: 190098833x
Grades 3–7
   Containing a wealth of knowledge for younger readers regarding the Arabian Peninsula. This encyclopedia is an asset; very interesting and easy to understand. This book is well organized with vivid illustrations. Covers topics such as: the past history, the traditional life, flora and fauna, and

modern Arabia. Includes a beautiful map of the Arabian Peninsula, a glossary and an index. Strongly recommended for middle school libraries.

196 *A Glossary of Islamic Terms*
Bewley, Aisha Abdurrahman.
London: Ta-Ha, 1998. 283 pp.
ISBN: 1897940785; ISBN (pbk.): 1897940726
General Readers

Instead of arranging the book as an alphabetical dictionary, which is a common practice, this book is divided into various key topics. As a result, the reader may approach the book in two ways. First, there is an alphabetical index by which a particular word can be located; second, the reader can go directly to the section of his or her interest to find the relevant material all in one place. The sections that deal with specific topics also mention some major figures and sources related to the topics being dealt with. Includes a "transliteration" page. A useful tool for those who wish to get information on specific topics in Islamic terms.

197 *The Oxford Dictionary of Islam*
Esposito, John L.
New York: Oxford University Press, 2003. 359 pp.
ISBN: 0195125584
General Readers

This dictionary is designed for general readers with little or no knowledge of Islam. It is organized in an easy-to-use, A-to-Z format, and provides more than two thousand entries. Uses cross references to guide readers to related discussions elsewhere in the volume. Many entries on topics of current interest, such as the Taliban, terrorism, Osama bin Laden and al-Qaeda are included in this volume. "Although the focus is on the nineteenth and twentieth centuries, the inclusion of important persons and places in the history of Islam broadens the scope of the work." —*Booklist*

198 *The Junior Encyclopedia of Islam*
Khan, Saniyasnain.
New Delhi: Goodword Kidz, 2003. 2003 pp.
ISBN: 8187570741
Grades 7–12

An excellent resource for any library. It covers topics such as introduction to Islam, What is Islam? What do Muslims believe? Who was the Prophet Muhammad? What is the Qur'an? What is the Ka'bah? How do

Muslims practice their faith? Arabic writing, world's Muslim population, What is jihad? The Islamic calendar, ten masterpieces of classical Islamic art, A–Z fact finder, chronology of Islam, notable Muslims, prayers from the Qur'an, and prayers from the Hadith. One can get a fairly good grasp of the basic information regarding Islam after using this encyclopedia. Although this book is designed for junior high school students, it can be very useful for any one who wishes to get an overview of Islam in a simplified and interesting manner. A few colored illustrations, including a sample of some prayers from the Qur'an in Arabic (surahs) followed by English translation, and a list of books "suggested for further reading" are included.

199 *A Basic Dictionary of Islam*
Maqsood, Ruqaiyyah Waris.
Lahore, India: Talha Publication, 2001. 239 pp.
Grades 7–10

It is a very useful resource to help understand the meaning of commonly used terms in Islam. The definitions of words are easy to understand, and are explained in paragraphs instead of just a few words like some other dictionaries. When necessary, the dictionary also has some cross-references. Includes black-and-white illustrations.

200 *A Popular Dictionary of Islam*
Netton, Ian Richard.
Atlantic Highlands, New Jersey: Humanities Press International, 1992. 279 pp.
ISBN: 0391037560
General Readers

This compilation is a dictionary as well as a glossary of terms. It contains brief biographies of prominent Muslims and Islamic scholars throughout the ages. Cross references within entries are printed in bold type. This dictionary contains terms which the reader is likely to encounter in current reading on the subject of Islam. "Guide to further reading" covers ten pages. It is source that should be useful to layman, student, scholar, and Muslim and non-Muslims.

201 *A Concise Encyclopedia of Islam*
Newby, Gordon Darnell.
Oxford, England: Oneworld, 2002. 244 pp.
ISBN: 1851682953
Grades 10–12

This comprehensive encyclopedia, containing over one thousand entries, covers all the different branches and movements within Islam, including Shi'ite, Sufi, and Sunni traditions. Key historical moments, pinpointing important geographical locations are explained. Many of the terms are transliterated from their original scripts in the Islamic languages of Arabic, Persian, Turkish, and Urdu. This is an important reference tool which will be invaluable to high school students, scholars, and those who wish to learn and understand the heritage of Islam. Includes black-and-white photographs and a map, cross references, a chronology, a bibliography and an index. Well researched.

202 *Milet Mini Picture Dictionary*
Turhan, Sedat. Illustrated by Sally Hagin.
London: Milet, 2003. 48 pp.
ISBN: 1840593482
Grades K–3
Designed with preschoolers in mind, this is a vibrantly colored picture dictionary with Arabic and English words to help readers identify objects and words in the target language. Basic subjects included are plants, animals, shapes, food, home, school, clothing. It is available in twelve bilingual editions.

HISTORY AND POLITICS

203 *A History of the Arab Peoples*
Hourani, Albert Habib.
Cambridge, Massachusetts: Belknap Press of Harvard University Press,
        1991. 551 pp.
ISBN: 0674395654
General Readers
Albert Habib Hourani, a distinguished historian, has written an overview of Arab history and culture that encompasses from pre-Islamic Arabia to contemporary times such as the Palestinian question. This is truly an academic feat with a full range of issues in regard to all aspects of the Arab world. Includes black-and-white illustrations, maps, and an index. A valuable reference resource. "Written by a master historian, this work is now the definitive study of the Arab peoples."—*Library Journal*. "Hourani examines Arabic-speaking nations of the Islamic world from the seventh century to the present in a volume that spent twelve weeks on PW's bestseller list and was a History Book Club main selection."—*Publishers Weekly*

INTERRELIGIOUS STUDIES

204 *The Choice: Islam and Christianity*
Deedat, Ahmed.
Verulam, South Africa: A. Deedat, 1993. 228 pp.
General Readers
In 1985 Ahmed Deedat, the author of this book, received the King Faisal International Award for service to Islam. This book is aimed at promoting the religion of Islam against the distortions of the faith by Christians. Beliefs of Christianity and Islam are compared from the perspective of a Muslim. It would interest those who are seeking to learn about these two major religions of the world.

205 *Historical Atlas of Religions*
Farrington, Karen.
New York: Checkmark Books, 2002. 192 pp.
ISBN: 0816050694
Grades 7–12
This excellent tool containing a wealth of information about religions is essential for all libraries. The photographs, portraits, and maps, chiefly color, are extraordinary. Equally outstanding is the author's regional approach to the study of the major faiths of the world. The author demonstrates how beliefs of different cultures evolved, the spread of their influence, and areas of religious conflicts. Containing full-color maps and illustrations, it is a commendable atlas. The most coverage is given to Christianity, perhaps due to its historical influence on the people in many parts of the world. "The organization does not promote quick access to specific facts or significant dates and statistics, but there is an index. On the whole, Farrington's work presents more variety than Trevor Barnes's *The Kingfisher Book of Religions* (Kingfisher, 1999) and more substance than Anita Ganeri's *The Atlas of World Religions* (Peter Bedrick, 2001)."
—*School Library Journal*

ISLAMIC FAITH AND PRACTICE

206 *Islam Today: A Short Introduction to the Muslim World*
Ahmed, Akbar S.
London; New York: I. B. Tauris Publishers, 2002. 253 pp.

ISBN:1860642578
General Readers
This book arose out of a BBC television series. The first two chapters discuss the life of the Prophet Muhammad and the Qur'an's five pillars, which govern the beliefs and behavior of Muslims. The author, a distinguished anthropologist and a well-known authority on Islam, then sets out to bridge gulfs of misunderstanding regarding Islam. He explores issues such as how the great Ottoman, Safavid, and Moghul empires have deeply marked the successor states in Turkey, Iran, Pakistan, and India, and the plight of Muslim minorities in the West struggling to maintain their identities in hostile environments. Includes a glossary, a list of references, and an index. It is a useful book for students and general public alike. Recommended for any library collection. "Anthropologist Ahmed accurately explains the conflicting cultural values and ignorance of East and West, and does an excellent job explaining the differences between Shi'ite and Sunni branches of Islam, women in Islam, and Muslim minorities."
—*Library Journal*

207 *An Employer's Guide to Islamic Religious Practices*
Council on American-Islamic Relations.
Washington, D.C.: Council on American-Islamic Relations, 1997. 12 pp.
General Readers
A necessary booklet for anyone working with Muslims. Provides information regarding the United States's legal protection of religious practices of Islamic followers such as daily prayer, washing, prayer space, fasting, food, and so forth.

208 *Interpreting Islam*
Donnan, Hastings.
London: Sage Publications, c2002. 196 pp.
ISBN: 076195421x; ISBN (pbk.): 0761954228
General Readers
Containing a collection of articles by ten authors, this book provides an overview of Islam, which is one of the least understood religions in the West and surrounded by myths and stereotypes. It provides a penetrating guide to the diversity and richness of contemporary knowledge about Islam and Muslim society in general. Interdisciplinary in scope and organization, the book includes chapters that cover Islamic studies, sociology, politics, anthropology, and culture. Includes an index. A very valuable resource.

209 *Silent No More: Confronting America's False Images of Islam*
Findley, Paul.
Beltsville, Maryland: Amana Publications, 2001. 323 pp.
ISBN: 1590080009; ISBN (pbk.): 1590080017
General Readers

The author, a Christian and a former Illinois congressman, wrote this book to dispel the false stereotypes of Islam held by some Americans. His dedication to his friendship with many prominent Muslims throughout the world resulted in writing this book. A very enlightening read to gain a better understanding of Islam.

210 *What Is Islam? A Comprehensive Introduction*
Horrie, Chris and Peter Chippindale.
London: Virgin, 2003. 282 pp.
ISBN: 0753508273
General Readers

This revised and updated edition provides a comprehensive introduction for anyone interested in learning all aspects of Islam. It discusses the following topics: 1. Faith: the origins of Islam, with an explanation of the Qur'anic law (the Shari'ah), and how it is dispensed; 2. Islamic History: the major events of Islamic history; 3. Islamic Sects: a breakdown of the Islamic sects and an account of the rise of militant Islam in the twentieth and twenty-first centuries; 4. The Muslim world: a directory of Islamic nations in order of importance. A select bibliography and an index are included. Quite informative.

211 *Index Islamicus: A Bibliography of Publications on Islam and the Muslim World since 1906*
Roper, G. J., and C. H. Bleaney, editors.
Bethesda, Maryland: Cambridge Scientific Abstracts internet database service, 2003–.
ISBN: 13600982
General Readers

The international classified bibliography of publications in European languages on all aspects of Islam and the Muslim world. Described as "an indispensable tool for libraries, graduates and undergraduates alike," it provides the reader or a researcher with an effective overview of what has been published on a given subject in the field of Islamic Studies in its broadest sense. It includes extensive indices of names and subjects and reviews. This database is also available online, on the World Wide Web, as well as CD-ROM versions. Highly recommended for researchers.

212 *Elementary Teachings of Islam*
Siddiqui, Moulana Mohammed Abdul-Aleem.
Brentwood, Maryland: International Graphics Printing.
Grades 6–8
   Unless one is going to convert to Islam, this book is not appropriate for research. The intent of the author is to present the basic rudiments of Islam to recent Muslim converts and to be used as a handbook for Islamic schools that use English as the medium for instruction. Some of the text in this book is in English. Includes black-and-white photographs.

213 *Islam*
Williams, John Alden.
New York: George Braziller, 1962. 256 pp.
ISBN: 6115500
General Readers
   Although this book was published in 1962, it gives a thorough description of Islam. Includes references and notes, a guide to pronunciation of terms, and an index.

MUSLIM CULTURE AND CUSTOMS

214 *To Be a Muslim: Islam, Peace, and Democracy*
Hassan bin Talal, Prince of Jordan; in collaboration with Alain Elkann.
Brighton, England; Portland, Oregon: Sussex Academic Press, 2004. 82 pp.
ISBN: 1903900824
Grades 10–12
   Written in a question-and-answer format, this book promotes inter-faith dialogue, understanding of Islam, and world peace. Prince El Hassan of Jordan responds to forty-one questions in a very informative way. He argues that the beliefs and culture of the majority of the Islamic world are contributive to a world at peace. He also emphasizes that Islam has applied the teachings of the Prophet Muhammad to treat other faiths and cultures with respect, fairness, and tolerance. The author provides basic information and views about a possible future in which the Islamic world and the West can live together harmoniously. Includes an index and a list of books for "further reading." Highly recommended book for high school libraries.

215 *The Muslim Marriage Guide*
Maqsood, Ruqaiyyah Waris.
Beltsville, Maryland: Amana Publications, 2000. 143 pp.
ISBN: 091595799x
General Readers
The author, a leading British Muslim scholar, draws on Islamic sources of the Qur'an to explain the main emotional, social, and sexual problems that can affect relationships. Many practical ways to resolve marital problems and help husband and wife to live together and respect each other's rights are suggested. A very useful guide for Muslim couples, who are married or are planning to get married. The chapter, "A short A to Z of marriage" lists some commonly used words with definitions. Non-Muslims can also benefit from the twenty suggestions listed under the last chapter, "a few rules for a happy marriage." A very useful resource.

216 *The Muslim World*
Orens, Geoffrey.
Bronx, New York: The H. W. Wilson Co., 2003. 199 pp.
ISBN: 0824210190
Grades 9–12
An excellent collection of articles and excerpts from books, etc. on topics of interest in regard to Islam. Older students or adults researching specific and current information will certainly be able to benefit by using this resource. Includes an index and a bibliography. Highly recommended.

RESISTANCE VERSUS TERRORISM

217 *Understanding September 11*
Calhoun, Craig, Paul Price, and Ashley Timmer, eds.
New York: New Press, c2002.
ISBN: 1565847741
General Readers
Contains a collection of chapters describing Islamic radicalism, globalization, New War/New World Order, terrorism, Democratic virtues, and September 11, 2001, terrorist attacks.

218 *National Security: Opposing Viewpoints*
Cothran, Helen.
San Diego, California: Greenhaven Press, 2004. 208 pp.

ISBN: 0737716959; ISBN (pbk.): 0737716967
General Readers

A collection of articles concerning the national security of the United States, written by experts, policy makers, and concerned citizens provides the reader with a wide diversity of opinions. The topics include threats to United States national security, ways to enhance national security, suggestions for response to terrorism, and the threat to civil liberties by enhanced national security. Includes an index.

219 *Martyrs: Innocence, Vengeance, and Despair in the Middle East*
Davis, Joyce.
New York: Palgrave, 2003. 214 pp.
ISBN: 0312296169
General Readers

After 9/11, there were a number of questions that needed to be explored, such as: Did the United States face the same threat of suicide bombers and other acts of terrorism as Israel? Did 9/11 happen because of the U.S. support of Israel? Will the threat of terrorism persist even after the resolution of the Israel-Palestinian conflict? Through personal interviews of Islamic scholars around the world, Islamic teachings on martyrdom are analyzed. The author, a foreign editor at Knight Ridder newspapers, explores the lives and deaths of some of the people considered by Muslims to be legitimate martyrs. A thought-provoking book for those who wish to understand the causes of anti-Americanism, the violence and terror of the Middle East, and an analysis of the people behind jihad, martyrdom, and suicide bombing.

220 *The Middle East: Opposing Viewpoints*
Dudley, William.
San Diego, California: Greenhaven Press, 2004. 203 pp.
ISBN: 0737718056; ISBN (pbk.): 0737718064
General Readers

This book presents a wide diversity of articles regarding the Middle East, written by prominent experts, policy makers, and concerned citizens. The viewpoints discussed are the reason the Middle East is a conflict area, how Islam affects the Middle East, the role of the U.S. in the Middle East, and possible peace between Israel and Palestine. A wonderful resource to stimulate debate about this controversial subject. Includes an index.

221 *What Everyone Needs to Know about Islam*
Esposito, John

Oxford; New York: Oxford University Press, 2002. 204 pp.
ISBN: 0195157133
General Readers

The author wrote this book out of his experiences after the tragedy of 9/11. The primary focus of this book is to communicate Muslim beliefs and the reasons for these beliefs. Readers can get answers to specific questions of their interest in various subject areas of Islam. Each question and answer is self-contained. The book is very well organized, interesting, and simple to understand. It includes a glossary, "suggestions for further reading" and an index. ". . . [A]n excellent primer on all aspects of Islam."—*Publishers Weekly*

222 *Sami and the Time of the Troubles*
Heide, Florence Parry and Judith Heide Gilliland; illustrated by Ted Lewin.
New York: Clarion Books, 1992. [32] pp.
ISBN: 0395559642
Grades 3–6

This is a story about Sami, a ten-year-old Lebanese boy who lives with his widowed mother, his little sister, and his grandfather in Beirut, Lebanon. Due to the gunfire in the streets, they spend much of their time in the basement of an uncle's house. Sami remembers all the good times he and his family used to have before the bombing in the streets. Their basement is lined with glowing carpets that remind them of how beautiful life was before the fighting. Includes stunning watercolor illustrations. "Lewin's watercolor illustrations capture contemporary Beirut with stunning clarity and drama."—*School Library Journal*. "This uncommon picture book, valuable for its portrait of children caught in a modern-day conflict, is sure to lead to thought-provoking discussions."—*Publishers Weekly*

223 *The Day the Sky Fell: A History of Terrorism*
Meltzer, Milton.
New York: Random House, 2002. 290 pp.
ISBN: 037582250X; (pbk.)ISBN: 037582250X
Grades 6–10

Originally published in 1983 as *The Terrorist: The Day the Sky Fell,* this book provides information regarding the history of international terrorism. The award-winning author, Milton Meltzer, offers reaction, reflection, and some background information on September 11. By citing terrorist attacks that took place in various parts of the world throughout the ages, he shows that terrorism is as old as humankind. Black-and-white illustrations are included. "Discussion guides" for classroom use and Meltzer's answers to questions posed about the writing of each of his books, should be very helpful for readers. A bibliography and an index are included. "A worthy asset for any library."—*School Library Journal.* "A carefully researched, timely book on a subject of tragically crucial importance."—*The Horn Book Magazine*

224 *Osama's Revenge: The Next 9-11: What the Media and the Government Haven't Told You*
Williams, Paul L.
Amherst, New York: Prometheus Books, 2004. 261 pp.
ISBN: 1591022525
General Readers
    Dr. Williams, who once served as a consultant for the FBI, openly discusses Osama bin Laden's hatred of the United States, Jewish states, and Christians. Within each chapter, bin Laden's writings are translated. These writings are warning of the evils of the U.S., and encouraging Muslims to fight. According to the author, Al Qaeda has accessed nuclear weapons created during the Cold War, and has plans to create a nuclear holocaust in America. Includes black-and-white photographs and an index. Highly recommended for those who are interested in learning more about the subject of terrorism and resistance against the West.

7

Geography

This chapter lists twenty resources to introduce various Muslim countries. Of these resources, one resource is for the high school, seventeen for the middle school, and two are for the elementary school grade levels. Information regarding culture, government, maps, industry, economy, and agriculture is provided.

225 *Qatar*
Augustin, Byron; and Rebecca A. Augustin.
New York: Children's Press, 1997. 128 pp.
ISBN: 0516203037
Grades 5–9
One of the titles from the series "Enchantment of the World," this is a fascinating and invaluable resource to provide young readers information regarding Qatar, a very small Middle Eastern country located along the western coast of the Persian Gulf. This book discusses the history, geography, culture and family life, plants and animals, economy and industry, government, education, and art of Qatar. The text is complemented by beautiful color photographs and maps. "Mini-facts at a Glance" and "Important Dates" at the end summarize important information and time periods covered in the book regarding Qatar. A list of "Important People" and an index are included as well. An excellent book on this subject, and highly recommended for school libraries.

226 *United Arab Emirates*
Augustin, Byron.
New York: Children's Press, 2002. 144 pp.

ISBN: 0516204734
Grades 6–9

The United Arab Emirates, a crescent-shaped country located in the southeastern corner of the Arabian Peninsula, is the subject of this fascinating book, which is also a part of the series titled "Enchantment of the World, Second Series." The author explains in a very interesting manner, the geography, history, vegetation and animals, archaeology, government, agriculture and industry, and culture in the United Arab Emirates. Old and new traditions among families of the United Arab Emirates are explained, such as selecting a spouse, women in society, unique sports such as camel racing, traditional dresses, and food. The "Timeline" and "Fast Facts" at the end of the book summarize all the important facts and events covered in the book. Excellent color photographs and maps make this book even more interesting and informative. Includes an index. Highly recommended for school libraries. "A solid addition for most collections."
— *School Library Journal*

227 *Syria*
Beaton, Margaret.
Chicago: Children's Press, 1988. 125 pp.
ISBN: 0516027085
Grades 5–9

Syria, an ancient land on the eastern shore of the Mediterranean Sea, has been a gateway between Asia, Europe, and Africa for thousands of years. Part of the series titled "Enchantment of the World," this volume discusses the geography, the history, the religion, and the everyday life of people of Syria. Includes "Mini-Facts at a Glance," "Important Dates," "Important People," and an index. The color photographs and maps are very effective. An essential resource with a wealth of information. Highly recommended for school libraries. "Excellent sources for report material. Can help to contribute to greater understanding of life and social conditions."— *School Library Journal*

228 *Egypt*
Cross, Wilbur.
Chicago: Children's Press, 1982. 124 pp.
ISBN: 051602762x
Grades 5–9

Similar to other titles in the series "Enchantment of the World," this fascinating book covers a great deal of information regarding the geography, the history, life in modern Egypt, industry and agriculture, the arts and education, and people and customs of Egypt. Includes a list of "Cities and Towns in Egypt," "Mini-Facts at a Glance," "Important Dates," "Important People," and an index. Color maps and photographs complement the text. Highly recommended for school libraries.

229 *Afghanistan*
Englar, Mary.
Mankato, Minnesota: Capstone Press, 2004. 64 pp.
ISBN: 0736821740
Grades 4–6

A good choice for reluctant readers in that every other page has a colorful picture. The topic headings are in large bold print, and the information is concise, often enhanced with "fast fact" boxes. An excellent introduction to climate, landforms, wildlife, history, government, economy, traditions, culture, and the people of Afghanistan. Discusses how the people from Afghanistan are trying to rebuild their country from the ground up. Includes a historical timeline, "Words to Know," an index, and even a traditional recipe. Very timely and interesting book for children who want to get basic information regarding Afghanistan. Highly recommended for school libraries.

230 *Iraq*
Foster, Leila Merrell.
New York: Children's Press, 1998. 144 pp.
ISBN: 0516205846
Grades 5–9

One of the titles from the series "Enchantment of the World," this is an exceptionally invaluable resource for young readers who wish to learn about Iraq, formerly known as Mesopotamia, and a country where much of civilization began. Among many topics, the author presents the history, geography, family and tribe, Islam's influence, culture, agriculture, archaeology, and industry. The last two chapters are titled "An Iraqi's World," and "An Iraqi Youngster's Day," which describe some of the Iraqi customs, sports, arts, and traditions. The text is complemented by beautiful color photographs and maps. Like many of Foster's other books in this series, this book also includes very helpful "Timeline" and "Fast Facts" that summarize important information about Iraq. An excellent book for youngsters to learn about this region that is so much on the news. Includes an index.

231 *Jordan*
Foster, Leila Merrell.
Chicago: Children's Press, 1991. 128 pp.
ISBN: 0516026038
Grades 5–9
From the series titled "Enchantment of the World," this publication in an excellent introduction to Jordan, an Islamic country in the southwestern part of Asia, which borders Israel to the west, Syria to the north, Iraq to the east, and Saudi Arabia to the southeast and the south. In addition to describing the history and geography of Jordan, the author discusses King Hussein's reign from 1950 to 1991; Jordanian society, which includes government, religion, education, the arts; agriculture, industry, mining, transportation, and economy. Tribes and family life among the Jordanians, and the famous sites in Jordan are discussed in the last two chapters. Beautiful color photographs and maps complement the text. "Mini-Facts at a Glance" is a very helpful section at the end, which provides the summary of important information contained in the book. Includes an index. Highly recommended for school libraries.

232 *Kuwait*
Foster, Leila Merrell.
New York: Children's Press, 1998. 143 pp.
ISBN: 0516206044
Grades 5–9
One of the titles from the series "Enchantment of the World, Second Series" it is an invaluable and fascinating resource to introduce young readers to Kuwait, an oil-rich country located on the northwestern shore of the Persian Gulf. The book discusses the history, geography, economy, language, religion, sports, arts, and culture of Kuwait. Using fictional characters, the author writes accounts of what happened to Kuwait during Desert Storm. Contains beautiful color photographs, maps, a "Timeline," handy "Fast Facts," a list of additional resources, including the Internet, and an index. It is a well-researched and very interesting and informative book that is highly recommended for school libraries.

233 *Lebanon*
Foster, Leila Merrell.
Chicago: Children's Press, 1992. 127 pp.
ISBN: 0516026127; ISBN (pbk.): 0516026011
Grades 5–9

Another title from the series "Enchantment of the World," this is an exceptionally well-written and -researched resource about Lebanon, a country on the shores of the Mediterranean Sea. The first six chapters out of the nine chapters describe the geography and history of Lebanon: ancient Lebanon (prehistory to 560 AD); Arab conquest of Independence (history from 636 to 1941); years of conflict and years of chaos from 1941 until the present. The author also discusses the government, family, culture, education, agriculture, industry, economy, and tourism in Lebanon. Includes an index, beautiful color photographs and maps, "Mini-Facts at a Glance," "Important Dates," and "Important People." A very interesting and informative resource for learning about Lebanon. Highly recommended for school libraries.

234 *Oman*
Foster, Leila Merrell.
New York: Children's Press, 1999. 144 pp.
ISBN: 0516209647
Grades 5–9
The author, who has written many other books in the series titled "Enchantment of the World: Second Series," introduces the young readers to another Middle Eastern country, Oman, which is situated on the eastern part of the Arabian Peninsula. The author provides information regarding the history, geography, plants and animals, trades, government, education, industry, agriculture, as well as the culture in Oman. A very interesting chapter titled "A Visit to an Oman Family" discusses the activities that take place on a typical day of one Omani family. The last section, "Timeline" and "Fast Facts," summarize all the important dates, events, and facts mentioned in the book. Beautiful color photographs complement the text. A list of additional resources, including some websites, and an index are included. Highly recommended for school libraries.

235 *Saudi Arabia*
Foster, Leila Merrell.
Chicago: Children's Press, 1993. 127 pp.
ISBN: 0516026119
Grades 5–9
Saudi Arabia, the largest country on the Arabian Peninsula, where great deserts cover vast oil reserves, where Muslim pilgrims come to the holy cities of Mecca and Medina, and where the Arab peoples' movement to other countries began, is discussed in this series titled "Enchantment of the World." The author explores the history, including the kingdom of Saudi

Arabia, geography, industry, agriculture, economy, education, the arts, and family values and culture. The last chapter in this book is devoted to explaining the "Hajj," the holy pilgrimage and one of the five pillars of Islam in a very interesting and simple way. Beautiful color maps and photographs complement the text. "Mini-Facts at a Glance" summarize the important information and dates covered in the book. Includes an index. It is an excellent resource for school libraries. Highly recommended.

236 *Bahrain*
Fox, Mary, Virginia Fox.
Chicago: Children's Press, 1992. 126 pp.
ISBN: 0516026089
Grades 5–9
Part of the series titled "Enchantment of the World," this volume discusses the history, geography, culture, government, sacred objects such as pearls, agriculture, industry, religion, and the people of Bahrain, situated in the Persian Gulf. Fascinating color photographs and maps add visual introduction to this very interesting country. Includes "Mini-Facts at a Glance," "Important People," and an index. Very informative and highly recommended for school libraries.

237 *Iran*
Greenblatt, Miriam.
New York: Children's Press, 2003. 144 pp.
ISBN: 0516223755
Grades 5–9
One of the titles from the series "Enchantment of the World, Second Series," this is an invaluable and a fascinating book to acquaint children with the geography, plants and animals, history, economy, language, religion, culture, sports and arts, and people of Iran. "Timeline" covers important dates of Iranian history and world history; and the "Fast Facts" section contains a wealth of information regarding various aspects of Iran. Includes color photographs and an index. A very useful and interesting resource for children. Highly recommended for school libraries.

238 *Afghanistan: A True Book*
Heinrichs, Ann.
New York: Children's Press, 2003. 47 pp.
ISBN: 0516227750
Grades 3–6

Written by a regional and national award winning author, this is a fascinating book which discusses the geography, history, people, and culture of Afghanistan. It includes attractive color photographs, a map of Afghanistan, a list of Afghanistan organizations, additional book resources, online sites, a list of "Important Words" and an index. Highly recommended for elementary school libraries.

239 *Saudi Arabia*
Heinrichs, Ann.
New York: Children's Press, 2002. 144 pp.
ISBN: 0516222872
Grades 3–8
History, geography, government, religion, and the culture of Saudi Arabia are examined in this book. It is part of the series titled "Enchantment of the World, Second Series." Contains color photographs, maps, index, and bibliographic references.

240 *Islam: Faith, Culture, History*
Lunde, Paul.
London: Dorling Kindersley, 2003. 186 pp.
ISBN: 1405304049
Grades 6–8
This is a beautifully illustrated book which is a must for any educator or library. It provides a geographical, historical, and cultural understanding of the Islamic faith. Includes color pictures, maps, and an index. Easy and enjoyable reading.

241 *The Land and People of Malaysia and Brunei*
Major, John S.
New York: HarperCollins, 1991. 248 pp.
ISBN: 0060224886; ISBN (pbk.): 0060224894
Grades 6–10
Part of the series titled "Portraits of the Nations," this is an excellent book for introducing Malaysia and Brunei, prominent Muslim countries. The author introduces the history, geography, people, culture, government, and economy of the two nations, which are a very little known part of the world. It is an enlightening book that includes black-and-white pictures, maps, bibliographical references and an index. "There is something for all inquisitive readers in these pages."—*School Library Journal*

242 *Indonesia*
McNair, Sylvia.
Chicago: Children's Press, 1993. 126 pp.
ISBN: 0516026186; ISBN (pbk.): 0860371301
Grades 5–9

Part of the series titled "Enchantment of the World," this book introduces the geography, history, commerce and industry, agriculture, animal and bird life, religion, arts and crafts, and people and culture of Indonesia, a vast country, spread over thousands of islands. All the information is provided in a very organized and interesting manner, using fascinating color photographs and maps. Like the rest of the titles in this series, this book provides a summary of the facts in a section at the end titled "Mini-Facts at a Glance," which also includes important dates and important people. A very interesting resource with all the necessary information regarding this beautiful country.

243 *Turkey*
Orr, Tamra.
New York: Children's Press, 2003. 144 pp.
ISBN: 0516226797
Grades 5–9

A fascinating book that is part of the series titled "Enchantment of the World, Second Series." It discusses the geography, plants, animals, history, economy, language, religions, culture, sports, food, arts, and people of Turkey. Beautiful color photographs and maps will enable a reader to get a highly visual introduction to this very interesting country. Lists Turkish holidays, a timeline, "Fast Facts," a section that lists additional resources including Internet sites, and an index. A truly excellent resource with a lot of information about Turkey. Highly recommended for school libraries.

244 *Geography of the Muslim World*
Rahman, Mushtaqur, and Guljan Rahman.
Chicago: IQRA International Education Foundation, 1997. 319 pp.
ISBN: 1563163721
Grades 11–12

Written specifically for senior level school students, or any interested reader seeking knowledge about the geography of the Muslim countries, this very interesting book offers a wealth of basic information about 49 Muslim countries. Although diverse in cultures, languages, and environments, these countries have one aspect in common—their faith of Islam.

The introductory chapter in the book describes the rise of Islamic civilization, the basic principles of the Islamic faith, and the Islamic period from 634 AD to 1900 AD. Each of the chapters has been organized alphabetically by country, providing a short introduction, followed by essential coverage of its unique history, government, politics, economics, ethnicity, and much more. Each chapter includes a brief "Geographical Profile." Color photographs and maps are included as useful instructional aids. It is a highly recommended book for Muslims as well as non-Muslims to get a better understanding of all these Muslim countries around the world. Includes a "Selected Bibliography."

8

History and Politics

In this chapter one will find thirty-one resources describing the origins of Islam and its spread from its establishment to the present: sixteen resources are for the high school, eleven for the middle school, and four for the elementary school grade levels. Prominent historical and political events such as the Era of Crusades, the Mongol Period, and the Ottoman Empire, are included.

245 *The Crusades*
Biel, Timothy L.
San Diego, California: Lucent Books, 1995. 128 pp.
ISBN: 1560062452
Grades 6–8
   Provides a well-researched, detailed account of the era of the crusades from the beginning in 1096 AD to 1270 AD. This book should appeal to middle school students due to its conversational style and it includes many pictures for discussion of historical figures and events. Includes black-and-white illustrations, maps, a list of books for further reading, and an index. Richly informative.

246 *The Cross & the Crescent: A History of the Crusades*
Billings, Malcolm.
New York: Sterling Publishing Company, 1988. 239 pp.
ISBN: 0806969040
Grades 9–12
   Often the crusades have been glorified through history books, but the author of this book reveals the truth of life during the five centuries of the Holy War. New documents, detailed maps, and photographs depict the

horror and brutality of this era. Includes a bibliography and an index. Highly recommended.

247 *The Crusades: Failed Holy Wars*
Cartlidge, Cherese.
San Diego, California: Lucent Books, 2002. 112 pp.
ISBN: 156006996
Grades 8–12
    The crusaders thought the Muslims were "enemies of Christ" and that it was their sacred duty to retake the Holy Land, the place where Christ lived and died. Between 1096 and 1270 AD, there were eight major crusades. The crusaders failed to achieve their wish, but contact between the East and the West led to many cultural, political, and economic changes in Europe. Includes a chronology, a glossary, and an index. An enlightening account of the crusaders and their campaigns against the Muslims. "The black-and-white reproductions tend to be small and grainy and add little to the text. Overall, though, this is a worthwhile addition." — *School Library Journal*

248 *The Rise of Islam*
Child, John.
New York: Peter Bedrick Books, 1993. 64 pp.
ISBN: 0872261166
Grades 6–9
    Who are the historical figures associated with the Islamic religion? The author introduces each one of these prominent figures with relevant background material in regard to the historical time era. Prophets, holy men, and generals who have ruled and impacted events for 1,500 years and influenced the world are discussed in this book. Events that shaped history are explained in an easily understandable manner. Includes color illustrations, bibliographical references, maps, and an index. Very educational and interesting book for Muslims as well as non-Muslims. "Good overview to help students become acquainted with this religion, learn how it evolved into what we know it to be today, and understand how it has interacted with Christianity throughout the ages." — *School Library Journal*. "One element that doesn't work very well is the sidebar quotes from primary and secondary sources. Both in content and design, they are often distracting. Still, strictly as a historical overview, this is a book that should find a place on religion shelves." — *Booklist*

249 *The Islamic World: From Its Origins to the 16th Century*
Colombo, Monica.

Austin, Texas: Raintree Steck-Vaughn, 1994. 72 pp.
ISBN: 0811433285
Grades 9–12

Beautifully illustrated in color, this book examines the development of culture, the arts, economy, government, and Islamic religion throughout the world since the beginning of civilization to the end of the sixteenth century. Recreation of the life and times of people from various continents and cultures provides the basis for a global perspective that demonstrates how different civilizations and peoples around the world have influenced each other during the centuries. Includes maps, a glossary, and an index. Very informative and interesting. Highly recommended for high school libraries.

250 *The Medieval World*
Corbishley, Mike; illustrated by James Field.
New York: Peter Bedrick Books, 1992. 64 pp.
ISBN: 0872263622
Grades 5–7

Divided into seven chapters, and arranged in time sequence from 450 AD to 1500 AD, this book is an introduction to the greatest events in the world history from the end of the Roman empire in western Europe to the first voyages of Europeans to the New World of the Americas. Each chapter gives an overview of world events, important civilizations and major battles. In addition, it discusses the rise of the Islamic religion, the Vikings and the Medieval town. Beautifully illustrated and well organized, it also includes maps, diagrams, two time charts, and a glossary. A highly recommended book for school libraries.

251 *India in the Islamic era and Southeast Asia (8th to 19th Century)*
Dolcini, Donatella and Francesco Montessoro; illustrations by Giorgio Bacchin and Gianni de Conno.
Austin, Texas: Raintree Steck-Vaughn, 1997. 72 pp.
ISBN: 0817240950
Grades 10–12

A fascinating book that provides an overview of the history of India and Southeast Asia, with an emphasis on the development of Islam. It examines the arts, the culture, economy, government, and religion in those areas. Beautiful colored illustrations, chronological tables, a glossary and an index are included. An excellent resource.

252 *The Spread of Islam*
Dunn, John.

San Diego, California: Lucent Books, 1996. 128 pp.
ISBN: 1560062851
Grades 6–9

The author describes the origins of Islam and the fundamentals of this new faith. In order to understand Islam, it is also necessary to realize that after Muhammad's death two major Islamic sects arose from a dispute. These were the Sunnis and the Shi'ites. The Abbasid Golden Age and Islam's Medieval Empires, Imperial Islam in Decline, and Islam in Modern Times. are other significant chapters. Includes an index and black-and-white illustrations, including maps. A wonderful historical resource for school libraries. "While thorough and useful for reports, this detailed history of Islam is flawed in its presentation."—*School Library*

253 *The March of Islam: Time Frame AD 600–800*
Editors of Time-Life Books.
Alexandria, Virginia: Time-Life Inc., 1998. 176 pp.
ISBN: 0809464217
Grades 6–12

In addition to describing the history of the rise of Islam, this beautiful book also covers the historical events in Europe and Byzantium, India, China, and Southeast Asia as well as Japan. It provides readers an overall perspective of the 600–800 AD time era. Includes colored maps, pictures, illustrations, and an index.

254 *What Life was Like in the Lands of the Prophet: Islamic World. A.D. 570–1405*
Editors of Time-Life Books.
Alexandria, VA: Time-Life Inc., 1999. 144 pp.
ISBN: 0783554656
Grades 8–12

This book is an essential resource containing a wealth of historical information presented in an interesting format and supplemented by colorful illustrations and photographs. It is exceptional in that the historical figures and events described can excite one's imagination. Includes color pictures, a bibliography, an index, and a glossary.

255 *Glimpses of Islamic History*
Faqih, Irfan.
Lahore, India: Kazi Publications, 1979. 315 pp.
Grades 6–8

This book is primarily for readers interested in Islamic history and those who desire to learn about the origin and growth of political institutions in Islam. Divided into four distinct periods of Islamic history, it is a fairly good resource for insight into Islamic history. Includes a bibliography and an index.

256 *The Golden Age of Islam*
George, Linda S.
New York: Benchmark Books, 1998. 80 pp.
ISBN: 076140273x
Grades 9–12

The author explores a golden age in history that stretched from the last years of the eighth century to the middle of the thirteenth century C.E. The rise of Islam, beliefs and society, and the legacy of Islam's Golden Age are discussed. A chronology of the Golden Age of Islam, a glossary, a bibliography, and an index are included. Color photographs complement the text. A delightful book to arouse students' interest in history. "A very attractive, informative history of Islamic civilization from the eighth to the thirteenth century." — *Middle East Resources*

257 *Stories of Sirah*
Ghazi, Abid Ullah and Tasneema Khatoon Ghazi.
Chicago: IQRA International Educational Foundation, 1988–1998. 11 booklets
Grades 4–7

This is a set of eleven booklets which comprise the series "Stories of the Sirah." The stories are excellent depictions of the society in ancient Arabia and the struggles faced by the Muslims. Highly recommended for parents, educators, and librarians to understand the history of the society. Includes black-and-white illustrations.

258 *The Sword of the Prophet: A History of the Arab World from the Time of Mohammad to the Present Day*
Goldston, Robert C.
New York: Fawcett Crest, 1981. 224 pp.
ISBN: 0449243931
Grades 10–12

Robert Goldston, a highly acclaimed author, traces the history of the Arab world from the time of Muhammad to 1979. The historical roots of great events and the people who participated in those events are clearly explained.

Includes maps, bibliographical references and an index. An important contribution to any high school library.

259 *The Dark Ages*
Gregory, Tony.
New York: Facts on File, 1993. 80 pp.
ISBN: 0816027870
Grades 7–12

Well researched, this book describes significant events and personages, key political and economic developments, and the critical forces that inspired change in institutions as well as the everyday life of people around the globe between about 400 and 1000 AD, often called "The Dark Ages." It explores the history of the world from the fall of Rome to the rise of Islam, and discusses areas such as Europe, the Mediterranean, the Far East, and the Americas. This book is well organized, allowing ease of access and depth of coverage on a wide range of fascinating topics and time periods. The text is supplemented by original art, full-color photographs, maps, and diagrams. Also included are a glossary, time charts, an index, and a list of resources for further reading. A very informative and interesting resource.

260 *The Taliban and Beyond: A Close look at the Afghan Nightmare*
Hussain, S. Amjad.
Perrysburg, Ohio: BWD Publishing, 2001. 139 pp.
ISBN: 0971072310
Grades 10–12

The author discusses the history of Afghanistan, the Soviet occupation in 1979, the civil war in 1990, and the rise of the Taliban. In addition, the author also brings Afghanistan's history to its present transition after the events of September 11, 2001, and the war against terrorism by the U.S. and its allies. A well-researched book which includes a glossary and photographs of some places in Afghanistan.

261 *Crusaders*
Jessop, Joanne; illustrated by Nic Spender.
New York: Bookright Press, 1990. 23 pp.
ISBN: 0531183246
Grades 3–4

Adapted especially for younger readers, the story of the Christian Crusaders, who were European soldiers, unfolds as they travel to the Holy

Land. In this period of history, the Saracens, who were a fierce tribe of Muslim Turks, controlled the Holy Land. The time period of the many different crusades was from 1095 until the last one in 1290. The benefits of the many crusades were the new ideas and discoveries adopted by the Europeans and taken back to their countries. Includes color illustrations, a glossary, and an index. An excellent resource.

262 *A Nation Challenged: A Visual History of 9/11 and Its Aftermath*
Lee, Nancy; Lonnie Schlein; Mitchel Levitas: Dan Barry.
London: Jonathan Cape, 2002. 240 pp.
ISBN: 0224069640
Grades 6–12
Containing a remarkable collection of color pictures and maps, this pictorial history book of 9/11 and its aftermath is fascinating. The color photographs alone are a source of visual communication of events and people's feelings. The accompanying text is clear and easy to read. Highly recommended for all school libraries.

263 *The Assassins: A Radical Sect in Islam*
Lewis, Bernard.
New York: Oxford University Press, 1987. 166 pp.
0195205502
Grades 11–12
Originally published in Great Britain, this is an authoritative account of history's first terrorists. They were members of an offshoot of the Shi'ite sect of Islam who were the first group to use planned, systematic acts of murder as a political weapon. The groups were established in Iran in the eleventh century, and later on spread into Syria during the twelfth century. Their ideas have influenced today's Muslim fundamentalists. A very comprehensive and readable book. Includes an index.

264 *Good Muslim, Bad Muslim: America, The Cold War, and the Roots of Terror*
Mamdani, Mahmood.
New York: Pantheon Books, 2004. 304 pp.
ISBN: 0375422854
Grades 11–12
The first chapter offers a critique of the cultural interpretations of politics. Then it proposes a different way of thinking about political Islam such as the development of different tendencies as well as the rise of terrorism.

The rest of the book explains how religious identities arose in a clash with Western power. The book provides an explanation of the U.S. policy toward the Muslim world, and the lies, stereotypes, and generalizations upon the policy's foundations. A very provocative reading. Includes an index. "Mamdani is searching for big ideas, not nuances, and in this he is successful, making his book an important contribution to the national discussion on terrorism and Islam." —*Publishers Weekly*

265 *Crusaders, Aztecs, Samurai: From AD 600 to AD 1450*
Millard, Anne; illustrated by Joseph McEwan.
Tulsa, Oklahoma: EDC Publishing, 1990. 32 pp.
ISBN: 0860201945
Grades 4–6
    First published in England, this wonderful picture book traces history from 600 AD to 1450 AD. Although other cultures are discussed, young readers interested in Islam will find useful information about the beginnings of Islam, the spread of Islam, wars between religions, how Muslim people lived and traded with other cultures. Includes color illustrations and an index. A valuable resource for a school library.

266 *The Rise of Islam*
Moktefi, Mokhtar; illustrated by Sedat Tosun; English translation by Nan Buranelli.
Morristown, New Jersey: Silver Burdett Press, 1986. 64 pp.
ISBN: 0382092759; ISBN (pbk.): 0382092767
Grades 11–12
    Originally published in France in 1985, and translated into English in 1986, this book has a wealth of information about the history of the rise of Islam. The introductory chapter formulates the first centuries of Islam. Beautifully illustrated in color, it enhances the chronicles of Islamic history and many contributions of Islam, such as the creation of irrigation and agricultural technology and the development of large urban centers. Includes color illustrations, a chronology, and an index.

267 *The Arabs: A Living History*
Musallam, Basim.
London, Wisconsin: Harvill Press Ltd., 1983. 211 pp.
ISBN: 0002720108
Grades 9–12

Preceding the publication of this book, there was a documented film series with the same title by John Keary. This book attempts to address what non-Arabs would like to know about Arabs, and what Arabs would like to know about non-Arabs from different perspectives. It is a well researched historical account of what Islam represents, who Arabs are, and their geographical locations, including prominent figures and events. Includes an index and some color illustrations. A must for educators and librarians.

268 *The Rise of Islam*
Powell, Anton; illustrated by Nigel Chamberlain and Richard Hook.
New York: Warwick Press, 1980. 44 pp.
ISBN: 0531091651
Grades 5–9

An extraordinary book chronicling the rapid expansion of the Islamic religion and its effect on the lives of the people exposed to it. A marvelous research tool for young people.

269 *Cambridge Illustrated History of the Islamic World*
Robinson, Francis, editor.
New York: The University of Cambridge, 1996. 328 pp.
ISBN: 0521435102
Grades 9–12

The editor and his team emphasize the widespread misunderstanding in the West as to what Islam really is and how both civilizations owe much to one another. An unusual feature in this book is the inclusion of special panel pages on influential issues, ideas, people, places, and events. Includes a reference guide, an index, a bibliography, a glossary, maps and color and black-and-white photographs. A must for high school libraries. "Accessible, interesting, and thorough, this volume serves students who want be more informed about a religion that is so often in the news."—*School Library Journal*

270 *The Ottoman Empire*
Ruggiero, Adriane.
New York: Benchmark Books, 2003. 80 pp.
ISBN: 0761414940
Grades 6–9

An engrossing historical text that traces the history of the Ottoman Empire from the populations' origin of Nomads of the steppes of Central Asia to rulers of most of the countries bordering the Mediterranean, Black, Red, and Caspian Seas. The author discusses topics such as the history, the cultural history, beliefs and society, and the legacy of the Ottomans that has influenced today's world. Includes: "The Ottoman Empire: A Time Line," color maps, a glossary, a bibliography, and a list of websites for additional information on the subject. Highly recommended.

271 *A Brief History of Islam*
Sonn, Tamara.
Malden, Massachusetts: Blackwell Publishing, 2004. 203 pp.
ISBN: 1405109025
Grades 11–12
An advanced comprehensive overview of the history of Islam from its establishment to the present. The book discusses the rise and fall of dynasties, clash of ideas, the relationship of Judeo-Christianity, division and reorganization, colonialism and reform, and finally the obstacles and prospects for Islamic reform. In addition to black-and-white maps and pictures, an index is included. Recommended for students in honors programs only.

272 *Islamic States in Conflict*
Spencer, William.
New York: F. Watts, 1983. 90 pp.
ISBN: 0531045447
Grades 9–12
The author describes the history of conflict among Middle Eastern tribes and nations before and since the birth of Islam. He discusses the present situation in the Middle East from the perspective of several Arab states (Iraq, Lebanon, Syria, Jordan, Saudi Arabia, Egypt, and Iran). In spite of the ethnic and cultural differences, historical rivalries, differing interpretations of Islam, and modern political disputes, the Islamic states are united due to their common faith in Islam, and their common need to establish themselves as truly independent nations, free from foreign influence in their affairs. Includes an index and a list of books for further reading. An interesting book with good information, but it is somewhat outdated.

273 *The Mongol Period: History of the Muslim World*
Spuler, Bertold; introduction by Arthur N. Waldron.
Princeton, New Jersey: Markus Wiener Publishers, 1969. 103 pp.
ISBN: 1558760792
Grades 11–12

Written by the renowned German historian Bertold Spuler (1911–1990), this English translation is essential to promote an understanding of the history of modern Eurasia by examining the influence of the Mongol empires on China, Russia, and India. The author gives a precise view of both the Mongols and the countries with which they had conflict. Includes dynastic tables, a bibliography, indices, black-and-white pictures, and a map. Requires advanced reading skills. "This volume is still one of the few studies to deal authoritatively, comprehensively, and clearly to the non-specialist, with the Mongols."—*Book News, Inc.*

274 *The Age of the Caliphs: History of the Muslim World*
Spuler, Bertold; introduction by Jane Hathway.
Princeton, New Jersey: Markus Wiener Publishers, 1969. 113 pp.
ISBN: 1558760954
Grades 11–12
Written by the late Bertold Spuler, one of the world's leading experts on Muslim history, this book has been translated from German into English. It would be a valuable resource for readers interested in the history of Muslim countries beginning with Rome and Persia and pre-Islamic Bedouins and ending with the fall of Baghdad to the Mongols and Granada to the Christians. Includes dynastic tables, a bibliography, indices, black-and-white maps, and black-and-white photographs. Appropriate for students with advanced reading skills who are highly motivated.

275 *The Spread of Islam*
Swisher, Clarice.
San Diego, California: Greenhaven Press, 1999. 240 pp.
ISBN: 1565109678; ISBN (pbk.): 156510966x
Grades 9–12
The five chapters in this book focus mainly on the major turning points in Islamic expansion. The introduction provides an overview of Islamic beliefs and practices and how and why the religion has spread. The other chapters are introduced with a brief summary of the contributing writer's main themes and insights. The topics deal with the East-West spread of Islam, the spread of Islamic art and thought, the spread of factions within Islam, and the modern-day resurgence of Islam. Well organized, the contents contain brief abstracts. Includes a glossary, a chronology, an appendix, an index, and a list of books for further research on the topics covered in the book. Very informative. ". . . [P]resents a view of Islam mainly through Western eyes."—*Booklist*

9

Interreligious Studies

This chapter includes twenty-two resources explaining the relationships and common principles among the world's major religions, including Christianity, Hinduism, Islam, Judaism, and Sikhism. Some of the resources discuss similarities and differences among these religions. Out of the total number of resources, one can be adaptable to all grade levels, eight are for the high school, three are for the middle school, and eleven are for the elementary school grade levels.

276 *Daughters of Another Path: Experiences of American Women Choosing Islam*
Anway, Carol Anderson.
Lee's Summit, Missouri: Yawna Publications, 2002. 215 pp.
ISBN: 0964716909
Grades 10–12
   This is a heartwarming story written by a non-Muslim mother, who relates her experiences in regards to her daughter who converted to Islam, and the journey of reconciliation and acceptance of her daughter's conversion. Why are some American daughters leaving Christianity for Islam, a religion that requires submission, discipline, and being "different"? What are their lives like as a result of that choice? How can non-Muslims relate to Muslims who are relatives, friends, and acquaintances? Questions such as these are addressed by the author. Portions of stories from fifty-three American-born women who have converted to Islam are included as well. Includes appendices that list survey questionnaires, a glossary, a bibliography, and an index.

277 *The Kingfisher Book of Religions: Festivals, Ceremonies, and Beliefs
      from Around the World*
Barnes, Trevor.
New York: Kingfisher, 1999. 160 pp.
ISBN: 0753451999
Grades 4–7

A fascinating resource with a wealth of information, this book is a marvelous guide to various religions in the modern world. It explains the origins, development, beliefs, festivals, and ceremonies of several world faiths
and where they are practiced. These include Hinduism, Buddhism, Judaism, Christianity, Islam, and traditional religions of Australian aborigines
as well as Native Americans. Color photographs, a glossary, and an index
are included. Highly recommended for junior high school libraries.
"Thoughtfully arranged in short chapters and brightly illustrated."—*School
Library Journal*

278 *Religions of the world: The Illustrated Guide to Origins, Beliefs, Tra-
      ditions & Festivals*
Breuilly, Elizabeth.
New York: Facts on File, 1997. 160 pp.
ISBN: 081603723x
Grades 7–12

A wonderful chapter in this book presents the essential facts concerning
Islam. The accompanying color photographs and maps complement the
text. The rest of the chapters in the book discuss other major religions of
the world. Includes an index. "The writing is scholarly, lucid, and nonpar-
tisan."—*School Library Journal*

279 *For Every Child: The UN Convention on the Rights of the Child in
      Words and Pictures*
Castle, Caroline.
New York: P. Fogelman Books, published in association with UNICEF,
      2001. 16 pp.
ISBN: 0803726503
Grades 1–3

This is an extraordinary text that can be easily understood by children. It
is illustrated with colorful drawings. Fourteen of the most important rights
of the fifty-four principles adopted by the UN Convention on the Rights of
the Child is a must for any librarian.

280 *Religious Costumes*
Galford, Ellen.
Broomall, Pennsylvania: Mason Crest, 2002. 64 pp.
ISBN: 1590844297
Grades 5–6

Examines religious costumes worn by followers of Christianity, Islam, Judaism, Hinduism, Sikhism, Buddhism, and Shintoism, and their use to perform sacred rituals and express spiritual beliefs and moral values. The author explains the symbolism of the garments worn during religious ceremonies, many of which have remained the same for hundreds of years. This book is complemented by fascinating color photographs.

281 *Growing Up: From Child to Adult*
Ganeri, Anita.
New York: Peter Bedrick Books, 1998. 30 pp.
ISBN: 0872262871
Grades 3–5

The author examines the rites and rituals that mark the transition from childhood to adulthood among the major religions: Hinduism, Buddhism, Sikhism, Judaism, Christianity, and Islam. Includes attractive color illustrations. "The information is presented in a clear, simple language and illustrated with bright, colorful photographs and drawings."—*School Library Journal*

282 *Journey's End: Death and Mourning*
Ganeri, Anita.
New York: Peter Bedrick Books, 1998. 30 pp.
ISBN: 0872262898
Grades K–3

The author discusses rituals and rites surrounding death among six major religions: Hinduism, Buddhism, Sikhism, Judaism, Christianity, and Islam. Each faith has its own beliefs about the afterlife as well as funeral customs and rituals. Includes bright, colorful photographs and drawings, fact file, glossary, and an index.

283 *New Beginnings: Celebrating Birth*
Ganeri, Anita.
New York: Peter Bedrick Books, 1998. 30 pp.
ISBN: 0872262863
Grades 3–5

Introduces rituals and celebrations regarding the birth of a newborn baby among six major world religions: Hinduism, Buddhism, Sikhism, Judaism, Christianity, and Islam. Popular names and significant birthdays are also included. Contains some color illustrations. "While the strength of the volumes is their cross-cultural scope, a major drawback is their overgeneralization. Only the introduction notes that customs vary in different parts of the world and that only some of them are being described in the book."
—*School Library Journal*

284 *The Prophets*
Ibrahim, Muhammad and Isa Musa.
London, England: IQRA Trust, 1992. 43 pp.
ISBN: 1856799018
Grades 1–2
An interesting educational tool for introducing four of the great prophets sent by Allah in different historical periods and countries. This is an excellent book to show the commonality between Islam and other major religions of the world. Includes color pictures and an index.

285 *Islam, Christianity, and Judaism*
Kavanaugh, Dorothy.
Broomall, Pennsylvania: Mason Crest Publishers, 2004. 120 pp.
ISBN: 1590846982
Grades 6–9
This is one of the four volumes in the series titled "Introducing Islam." The author examines the historical context in which Islam, Christianity, and Judaism developed. She also provides an overview of the important beliefs and religious practices expected of each faith's followers. Interaction among these three religions in both the ancient and modern worlds is discussed as well. Color maps and illustrations complement the text. Includes a chronology, a glossary, Internet resources, and an index. Highly recommended for school libraries.

286 *Riding the Fence Lines: Riding the Fences That Define the Margins of Religious Tolerance*
Keating, Bernie with Rabbi Gordon et al.
Toledo, Ohio: BWD Publishing, 2003. 180 pp.
ISBN: 0971072345
Grades 9–12

A fascinating book that educates the reader about Islam, Judaism, Buddhism, Catholicism, and Episcopalism. A very helpful book to help dispel stereotypes and myths about each of these religions.

287 *Religions, East and West*
Kettelkamp, Larry.
New York: Morrow, 1972. 128 pp.
ISBN: 0688200303; ISBN (pbk.): 0688300308
Grades 8–10
This book discusses how the world's principal religions originated, who the religious leaders were, and what work is being done today that will influence the faith of the future. The religions discussed are Hinduism, Buddhism, Taoism, Confucianism and Shintoism; Parsism, Christianity; and Islam. Similarities and differences among these religions are discussed as well. Includes some black-and-white illustrations and an index.

288 *The Greatest Stories from the Quran*
Khan, Saniyasnain.
New Delhi: Goodwordkidz, 2002. 72 pp.
ISBN: 8178980975
Grades 1–2
This a very useful book for children to realize the similarities between the stories in the Qur'an and the ones in the Christian Bible and the Jewish Torah. Text supported by color illustrations.

289 *Celebrations*
Kindersley, Anabel; photographed by Barnabas Kindersley.
New York: DK Publishing, 1997. 63 pp.
ISBN: 0789420279
Grades K–3
This wonderful text was written in association with UNICEF, the United Nations Children's Fund. A useful book for discussion on how Muslim holidays or festivals in Islam as well as in the other major religions of the world are observed and practiced. Color photographs, an index, and a calendar of celebrations are included.

290 *One God, Two Faiths: When Christians and Muslims Meet*
Klos, Sarah.
Cincinnati, Ohio: Friendship Press, 1989. 48 pp.

ISBN: 037700197x
Grades 9–12

This book consists of a suggested plan for a six-session study on Islam. In order to implement the program successfully, it is recommended to have a copy of the book titled *God Is One: The Way of Islam*. The program has been primarily designed to be used in a Christian educational setting; however, a variety of activities in this book enables the participants not only to come to clearer terms with their own Christian faith, but also to become informed about Islam. Suggested filmography should be very helpful in order to get maximum information. Christian educators particularly will find this source of more interest.

291 *Islam: An Introduction for Christians*
Martinson, Paul Varo; translated by Stefanie Ormsby Cox.
Minneapolis, Minnesota: Augsburg, 1994. 264 pp.
ISBN: 080662583X
Grades 10–12

Translated into English from German, the purpose of this book is to inform the Christian community about the faith of Islam. It is objective and impartial and remarkably clear. An extraordinary book for young people. Includes a glossary, an index, a brief bibliography and black-and-white photographs.

292 *Sacred Myths: Stories of World Religions*
McFarlane, Marilyn.
Portland, Oregon: Sibyl Publications, 1996. 101 pp.
ISBN: 0963832778
Grades 6–8

This well-illustrated book contains thirty-five of the best known and loved stories of seven of the world religions. The stories are taken from the mythic traditions of Buddhism, Christianity, Hinduism, Islam, Judaism, Native American, and Sacred Earth. By giving equal importance to each religion, the author conveys the message that there are many paths to truth and they all deserve respect. Inspiring and illuminating, the book provides brief explanation of each of the seven religions. Includes glossary of terms and pronunciation key. "An interesting, eclectic collection." —*Booklist*

293 *Great Religions of the World*
National Geographic Book Service.

Washington, D.C.: National Geographic Society, 1971. 420 pp.
ISBN: 0870441035
Grades 9–12

The publication date of 1971 does not detract from the simple, lovely color pictures and thorough examination of the major religions of the world. Fifty pages of the book are specifically regarding Islam. Very helpful resource for students to understand the common aspects of the major religions of the world. Includes color photographs and an index.

294 *Understanding Arabs: A Guide for Westerners. 3rd ed.*
Nydell, Margaret K.
Yarmouth, Maine: Intercultural Press, 2002. 218 pp.
ISBN: 877864153
Grades 9–12

An enlightening, easy-to-read book that provides a cross-cultural guide for foreigners who are living in an Arab country and are not familiar with Arab values, beliefs, and social practices, particularly the Westerners (North Americans and Europeans). It underlines the contrasts between Western and Arab societies. An invaluable guide for those who interact with Arabs. Includes bibliography and references for additional reading on the subject. "A rich resource for those who wish to better comprehend what they read and hear in the media."—*Midwest Book Review*

295 *One World, Many Religions: The Ways We Worship*
Osborne, Mary Pope.
New York: Alfred A. Knopf, 1996. 86 pp.
ISBN: 067993930x
Grades 4–7

The author discusses practices of worship in seven major religions in the world: Judaism, Christianity, Islam, Hinduism, Buddhism, Confucianism, and Taoism. Color photographs and black-and-white illustrations are included. It also has bibliographical references and index. "A solid overview of the world's major religions."—*School Library Journal*

296 *In the House of Happiness: A Book of Prayers and Praise*
Philip, Neil; illustrated by Isabelle Brent.
New York: Clarion Books, 2003. 1 v. (unpaged)
ISBN: 0618234810
Grades 1–12

This book contains a very delightful collection of fifty-eight short prayers representing major world religions: Buddhism, Christianity, Hinduism, Islam, and Judaism. Complemented by tribal chants, folk rhymes, and poems of praise, each page is artistically framed by a flowered border with gold edging. This book will help children appreciate the diversity of religions. Includes some color pictures. "This book offers the opportunity for quiet moments of reflection in a lovely setting."—*Booklist* "Pleasing to the eye."—*School Library Journal*

297 *God Is One: The Way of Islam*
Speight, R. Marston.
New York: Friendship Press, 1989. 139 pp.
ISBN: 0377001961
Grades 9–12

The author, a frequent participant in international conferences for dialogue between Muslims and Christians, writes, "It is important to know about Islam because that religion and way of life have provided important basic elements of modern civilization." He discusses who Muslims are, what their beliefs are, and how their faith shapes every aspect of their lives. He responds to questions such as: Who was Muhammad and what inspired him? What do Muslims believe about Christ? This book also discusses how closely Muslims and Christians resemble one another in their devotion to one God, and yet important issues of life and faith continue to divide the two groups. Includes a glossary and black-and-white illustrations, with examples of Islam's contributions in arts, science, medicine, and architecture to the world. Should be of great interest to readers interested in interfaith issues.

10

Islamic Faith and Practice

Due to the fact that there are many facets that would fall under this chapter, but with specificity, this chapter has been categorized into four major subsections; namely, Hadith, Holy Days, Muslim Culture and Customs, and Qur'an. This chapter contains eighty-four resources: twenty-six are for the high school, nine are for the middle school, and forty-nine are for the elementary school grade levels.

HADITH

Hadith is second in authority only to the Qur'an, and a record of the Prophet Muhammad's life, actions, and deeds. Unlike the Qur'an, the source of the teachings of the Hadith are not the direct word of God.

298 *A Manual of Hadith*
Ali, Muhammad.
New York: Olive Branch Press, 1988. 408 pp.
ISBN: 0940793202
Grades 11–12
   The Islamic Hadith refers to the traditions exemplified by the life of the Prophet Muhammad, founder of the Muslim religion. Each chapter presents Arabic and English summaries of the teachings of the verses from the Qur'an and Hadith.

299 *Glimpses of the Hadith*
Aziaullah, Muhammad.

Los Angeles: Crescent, 1980. 122 pp.
Grades 8–12

The Hadith, the records of the utterances, discourses, practices, usages, sayings, and the way of life led by Prophet Muhammad, is considered to be one of the fundamentals of Islamic belief, and is the subject of this book, which is divided into two parts. Part I defines Hadith, its practical value and importance to a Muslim. Part II discusses for the general reader the interpretation and the importance of a selection of Hadith categories and subjects. Includes quotations from the Hadith in Arabic.

300 *Glimpses of Life after Death: A Collection of Hadith on the Transition from This Life to the Hereafter, the Entrance to the Garden or the Fire*
Bah, Alpha Mahmoud.
New York: Writers Club Press, 2003.
ISBN: 0595267122
Grades 11–12

The main objective of this revised edition is to provide researchers with a scholarly collection of Hadiths, written record of the oral traditions passed down from Muslim to Muslim of what Muhammad was supposed to have said and done. The book contains seven chapters arranged into three parts. The first three chapters discuss life and death in the grave; chapters 4 and 5 discuss the Resurrection and Judgment processes; and chapters 6 and 7 present Paradise and Hell. The chapters are divided into sections and subsections with brief introductions. There are 257 Hadiths in this book, and they were retrieved by the author from the already existing easy-to-understand translations.

301 *Hadith, Traditions of Prophet Muhammad: An Introduction*
Doi, Abdur Rahman I.
Chicago, Illinois: Kazi Publications, 1980. 155 pp.
Grades 11–12

The Hadith gives a Muslim an embodiment of the code of life, and provides guidance in dealing with various issues, whether social, economical, political, and legal, or national and international. In this book, the author introduces Hadith according to the subjects and transliterates them immediately after giving the text. The transliteration will help those who do not know the Arabic language. This is a helpful resource particularly for English-speaking Muslims who wish to understand the "Message of the Prophet." Includes a "Select Bibliography."

302 *Amr and the Ants*
El-Magazy, Rowaa; illustrated by Stevan Stratford.
Leicester, England: The Islamic Foundation, 1999. 24 pp.
ISBN: 0860373304
Grades 4–5
A charming story, complemented by color illustrations, which teaches children the importance of respect for everyone, including a small creature such as an ant. The moral of the story represents one of the examples from the Hadith.

303 *A Visit to Madinah: The Prophet Muhammad for Little Hearts*
Khan, Saniyasnain; illustrated by Gurmeet.
New Delhi: Goodword Books, 2003. 23 pp.
ISBN: 8178982013
Grades K–5
The meaning and purpose of Prophet Muhammad's life and his teachings are explained. Contains beautiful illustrations.

304 *Animals in Islam*
Masri, Basheer Ahmad.
[s. l.]: Athene Trust, 1989. 250 pp.
ISBN: 187060301x
Grades 9–12
This book is very enlightening on the stance of the Islamic religion and its position on the treatment of animals. Not only are the views of the tenets of Islam are expressed, but views of other religions in regard to animals are discussed as well.

305 *Love Your Brother, Love Your neighbour*
Murad, Khurram.
Leicester, England: Islamic Foundation, 1982. 31 pp.
ISBN: 0860371158
Grades 5–6
This book contains six stories that demonstrate how people should relate to each other. Basic values such as love and sacrifice, charity and kindness, regard for rights, and being merciful can turn the task of living together joyfully.

306 *Hadith for Children*
Rauf, Abdur.
Des Plaines, Illinois: Library of Islam, 1987. 147 pp.

ISBN: 0933511140
Grades 5–7

This book is a collection of the Prophet's sayings. The author attempts to project simple and easy-to-understand traditions of the Holy Prophet as they pertain to children's everyday life. Hadith is necessary reading for all Muslim children; however, it would be a challenge to interest children of other faiths. This book is pertinent to those who are involved in Islamic education. The Hadith, which accompany the text, are given in Arabic and English. Contains black-and-white illustrations.

HOLY DAYS

The reader will find in this subchapter observance and celebration information of the major Muslim holidays, namely, Ramadan and Id al-Fitr.

307 *Muslim Festivals*
Ahsan, M. M.
Vero Beach, Florida: Rourke Enterprises, 1987. 48 pp.
ISBN: 0865929793
Grades 4–6

This book contains wonderful comprehensive descriptions of the customs of traditional Islamic festivals and celebrations. The origins and importance of Muslim festivals, the times of fasting and feasting, pilgrimage and prayers, and the giving of gifts are explained. Includes color photographs, a glossary, a bibliography, an index, and the Islamic calendar. It is well organized. Recommended for school libraries.

308 *The Three Muslim Festivals*
Ali, Aminah Ibrahim; illustrated by Aldin Hadzic.
Chicago: IQRA International Educational Foundation, 1998. 68 pp.
ISBN: 156316308x
Grades 4–6

A delightful collection of stories highlighting the three most important celebrations of Islam namely, Ramadan, Id al-Fitr, and Id al-Adha respectively. Traditions and practices tied to each of the three festivals are discussed. The author has presented the stories involving three main characters in a sensitive, engaging manner that will appeal to Muslims and non-Muslims. Color illustrations and a glossary are included. Highly recommended for school libraries.

309 *Ramadan*
Douglass, Susan L.; illustrations by Jeni Reeves.
Minneapolis, Minnesota: Carolrhoda Books, 2004. 48 pp.
ISBN: 0876149328
Grades 1–4

Well organized, this book provides young readers an excellent introduction to the Islamic observances during the month of Ramadan, and the customs practiced during the festival of Id al-Fitr. The text is complemented by effective color illustrations. It also includes a list of "new words" with pronunciations. A must for elementary school library collection. "The text and illustrations both emphasize the global reach of Islam portraying adults and children of many different backgrounds." —*Booklist*

310 *Zaki's Ramadhan Fast*
El-Moslimany, Ann Paxtonl; illustrated by Erica L. Butler.
Seattle, Washington: Amica Publishing House, 1994. 27 pp.
ISBN: 1884187080
Grades K–3

An appealing introduction to Ramadan, the month in which the Qur'an was revealed to the Prophet Muhammad. In this story, even though Zaki is not required to fast during Ramadan since he is a young boy, his parents and sister support him to achieve his goal of fasting for one day. He realizes that it takes a lot of effort and determination to fast. An excellent source to promote determination and goals for young people. Includes color pictures. "Excellent book for non-Muslim children to learn about the fast of Ramadan and Muslim children to see their lives depicted in mainstream literature." —K. Keyworth

311 *Muslim Festivals Throughout the Year*
Ganeri, Anita.
North Mankato, Minnesota: Smart Apple Media, 2004. 30 pp.
ISBN: 158340371x
Grades 4–6

By using color photographs and illustrations as well as some fun activities, Muslim festivals throughout the year are depicted in this book. The story behind each Muslim festival is explained, and a description of how each festival is celebrated around the world today adds to an understanding of Islam. A festival calendar and an index are included.

312 *Ramadan*
Ghazi, Suhaib Hamid Ghazi; illustrated by Omar Rayyan.

New York: Holiday House, 1996. 29 pp.
ISBN: 0823412547
Grades K–3

An appealing book for young children. The religious celebration of the month of Ramadan as practiced by Hakeem, a young Muslim boy, is described. Written in a clear informative style, the book is accompanied by warm, color illustrations that depict the joy of this holy day. The author gives just the right amount of background information, along with interesting details.

313 *Ramadan: A Muslim Time of Fasting, Prayer, and Celebration*
Gnojewski, Carol.
Berkeley Heights, New Jersey: Enslow Publishers, 2004. 48 pp.
ISBN: 0766022757
Grades 4–6

Author and storyteller Carol Gnojewski explains the rituals and traditions observed during Ramadan, a month-long observation of fasting and prayer among the Muslims. In this "Finding Out about Holidays" series, the importance of Ramadan to the Muslim people and how it can enrich their lives are also discussed. Beautiful color photographs, a map, and the Islamic calendar are very effective. "Ramadan Craft Project" and "Words to Know" at the end of the book should be very useful to promote classroom activities for young readers. Includes an index, some websites, and a list of books for additional information about Ramadan.

314 *Celebrating Ramadan*
Hoyt-Goldsmith, Diane; photographs by Lawrence Migdale.
New York: Holiday House, 2002 32 pp.
ISBN: 082341762x; ISBN (pbk.): 0823415813
Grades 4–6

Children can relate to a story about another child. As one reads this charming description of Ibraheem and his family, one can get a better understanding of Ramadan. The text is complemented by color illustrations, a glossary, and index and a very special cookie recipe usually baked for children is included. "Sensitive introduction to Ramadan . . . eloquent text."—*Booklist*

315 *My Id-ul-Fitr*
Hughes, Monica.

Chicago: Raintree, 2003. 24 pp.
ISBN: 141090640x
Grades 1–2

Beautifully photographed, this book discusses how one family celebrates Id al-Fitr, the most popular Muslim festival. The topics covered are the clothes, the food, the presents, and the celebration of this festival. Glossary and index are included.

316 *Better Than a Thousand Months: An American Muslim Family Celebration*
Jones-Bey, Hassaun Ali.
Fremont, California: Ibn Musa Publishing, 1996. 168 pp.
ISBN: 0965424804
Grades 4–6

This book is about an American Muslim family who is celebrating the holy month of Ramadan, one of the two major Muslim holidays. The book provides description of Islamic worship to a largely Christian and Western audience, while also helping Muslim families living in non-Muslim environments to better appreciate and explain to others about their religious rituals and the spirituality behind them. Includes Qur'anic calligraphy and landscape photography.

317 *Islamic Festivals*
Knight, Khadijah.
Crystal Lake, Illinois: Heinemann Library, 1997. 48 pp.
ISBN: 0431069646
Grades 4–7

Containing beautiful color photographs, this book introduces readers to the main Islamic festivals. Muslim children discuss their lives, what Islam means to them, and how they observe festivals celebrated in the Islamic faith. Includes an index and an Islamic calendar wheel showing some Islamic events in the lunar year.

318 *Ramadan and Id al-Fitr*
MacMillan, Dianne M.
Hillside, New Jersey: Enslow Publishers, 1994. 48 pp.
ISBN: 0894905023
Grades 3–4

Part of the series titled "Best Holiday Books," this book discusses the following topics related to the practice of Islam: breakfast before dawn;

Muhammad; the Five Pillars of Islam; mosques, minarets, and the Quar'an; Ramadan; and preparing for Id al-Fitr. Includes mostly black-and-white photographs, a glossary, and index. It is well organized and easy to read. "Although the writing is choppy, the texts are well researched and have a great deal of information."—*School Library Journal*

319 *Ramadan*
Marx, David F.
New York: Children's Press, 2002. [32] pp.
ISBN: 0516222694; ISBN (pbk.): 0516273779
Grades K–1
A charming, colorful easy-to-read book about the traditions of the Muslim fasting period, Ramadan. A wonderful resource for youngsters of all religions. "These simple introductions are just the right size and length to share with young children."—*School Library Journal*

320 *Majid Fasts for Ramadan*
Mathews, Mary: illustrated by E. G. Lewis.
New York: Clarion Books, 1996. 48 pp.
ISBN: 0395665892
Grades K–3
An eight-year-old boy wants to celebrate Ramadan as the older Muslims do by fasting. His family members oppose it because they feel that he is too young to fast. Complemented by color illustrations. "Excellent watercolor illustrations add to the charm of this book."—*Publishers Weekly*

321 *Id-ul-Fitr*
Merchant, Kerena.
Brookfield, Connecticut: Millbrook Press, 1998. 32 pp.
ISBN: 0761309632
Grades 3–5
The celebration of the most joyous festival in the Muslim calendar, Id al-Fitr, around the world is discussed. Five other Muslim festivals are also described briefly. Includes beautiful color photographs, index, glossary, and a list of other resources about Id al-Fitr. A must for elementary school libraries.

322 *Muhammadan Festivals*
Von Grunebau, Gustave E.; introduction by C. E. Bosworth.
London: Curzon, 1988. 107 pp.

ISBN: 0700702032

Grades 9–12

Muslim festivals and practices such as worship, the pilgrimage to Mecca, and fasting during Ramadan are discussed as typical elements of Islamic ritual. In addition to the physical attributes and the major events in the life of the Prophet Muhammad, the author also looks at the cult of local saints throughout the Islamic world.

323 *Ramadan*

Walsh, Kieran.

Vero Beach, Florida: Rourke Publishers, 2003. 24 pp.

ISBN: 1589522230

Grades K–3

Adapted especially for younger readers, this is a simply stated explanation of the traditions and festivities of the Muslim holiday, Ramadan. Colorful pictures complement the text. Includes a glossary and an index.

324 *Fasting and Dates: A Ramadan and Eid-ul-Fitr Story*

Zucker, Jonny; illustrated by Jan Barger.

Hauppauge, New York: Barron's, 2004. [16] pp.

ISBN: 0764126717

Grades K–2

A very appropriate introduction to the Islamic festival of Ramadan and Id al-Fitr for young children. With the help of delightful color illustrations, the author explains how a Muslim family fasts each day, goes to the mosque to pray, and enjoys a delicious feast to celebrate the festival of Id al-Fitr. The last two pages discuss the Five Pillars of Islam.

MUSLIM CULTURE AND CUSTOMS

The reader will find in this section resources that will provide an insight into the Islamic faith and practice, including the Five Pillars of Islam, clothing, Islamic marriage, death and much more.

325 *Understanding Islam and the Muslims*

Washington, D.C.: Embassy of Saudi Arabia, 1989. 27 pp.

Grades 7–9

Although containing only twenty-seven pages, this unique book addresses in a nutshell most of the very basic topics pertaining to Islam in a question-and-answer form. The following topics are covered: the Ka'bah, the five pillars of Islam, Prophet Muhammad, common origins of Islam and Christianity, contributions by Muslims and their effect on the world, women in Islam, Islamic marriage, death, cultural diversity reflected in mosque architecture, and some of the Islamic values and beliefs. Readers will find this book very useful because answers to all the basic questions are provided in a very simple and concise form. The color photographs are very effective. A couple of verses from the Qur'an are included as well. A highly recommended book for students as well as adults who wish to get basic information about Islam without spending too much time.

326 *I Am a Muslim*
Aggarwal, Manju; photography: Chris Fairclough.
London: Watts, 2001. 32 pp.
ISBN: 0749641754
Grades 3–6
   Islamic beliefs and family heritages are looked at through the eyes of an eleven-year-old young child. Topics covered by the author are Muslim law, inside the mosque, Muslim clothes, pilgrimage to Mecca, Muslim customs, the Muslim year, and Muslim facts and figures, It is an enjoyable and interesting book containing very effective color photographs. A glossary and an index are included. ". . . [G]ives a sense of how a religion affects the life of a single family." — *School Library Journal*

327 *Family Life in Islam*
Ahmad, Khurshid.
Leicester, England: Islamic Foundation, 1974. 32 pp.
ISBN: 0950395404
Grades 11–12
   The Islamic approach to life and society and the foundations on which the institution of family is structured is described. The objectives and functions of an Islamic family, its principles and rules are explored. In addition, the concept of marriage and family in Islam are examined.

328 *Islam*
Al Hoad, Abdul Latif.
New York: Bookwright Press, 1987. 48 pp.
ISBN: 0531180638
Grades 4–6

Introduction of Islam, its origins, growth, belief, and observances. Information on Islamic art, architecture, and customs is also provided. Color pictures, glossary, and an index are included. It is one of the series of books on religions of the world. ". . . [F]ull of color photos which add greatly to the information given." — *School Library Journal*

329 *The Beauty of Makkah & Madinah*
Amin, Mohamed.
Nairobi, Kenya: Camerapix Publishers International, 1999. 128 pp.
ISBN: 1874041539
Grades 10–12
The author narrates the history of Mecca and Medina and of the Islamic faith while explaining the significance of each shrine and its place in the performance of the pilgrimage, known as Hajj (one of the pillars of Islam). He also describes the Ka'bah which is central to the hearts of the world's Muslims, and is Islam's most holy shrine This book is a useful guide to those who cannot go to Mecca. Magnificent architecture and dramatic landscapes through the lens of world-renowned photographer Mohamed Amin, are captured in this book. Includes a glossary of terms and color photographs.

330 *Sufism: An Account of the Mystics of Islam*
Arberry, A. J.
Mineola, New York: Dover Publications, 2002. 141 pp.
ISBN: 0486419584
Grades 11–12
The topics covered in this book are the interpretation of the word of God, the life of the Prophet Muhammad, and the structure of Sufi theory and practice. This book will benefit those who are interested in mysticism, Islamic thought, and Muslim religious practices. Includes an index. Rather difficult to understand. "An excellent introduction to both the founders of Sufism and its basic foundations." — *Midwest Book Review*

331 *Thank You O Allah*
Bint Mahmood, Ayesha; illustrated by Asiya Clarke.
Leicester, England: Islamic Foundation, 2000. 19 pp.
ISBN: 0860373355
Grades K–1

Never-ending blessings by Allah evoke a child's feeling of thankfulness for everything that Allah has given, e.g., health, food, and life itself. Includes attractive color illustrations.

332 *What Muslims Believe*
Bowker, John.
Oxford, England: Oneworld Publications, 1998. 187 pp.
ISBN: 1851681698
Grades 11–12
Originally published as *Voices of Islam*, this book draws on interviews with Muslims across the broad spectrum of Islam, and provides an insight into the Islamic faith. Some of the most important issues covered are the interpretation of the Qur'an, the concept of Holy War, the role of women, and the scope of Islamic education. Includes a very helpful glossary and an index. Recommended for any high school and a college library collection.

333 *Who Are the Muslims?: Where Muslims Live, and How They are Governed*
Carr, Melissa S.
Broomall, Pennsylvania: Mason Crest Publishers, 2004. 120 pp.
ISBN: 1590847016
Grades 6–9
Complemented by color illustrations, this book provides a well-researched detailed account of who the Muslims are, an overview of the countries in which they live, their basic beliefs, and the history of the spread of Islam. The role of Islam in government and Islamic law including its importance, are also discussed in the book. Most current data are provided about the estimated 1.25 billion Muslims who live throughout the world currently. Includes a chronology, a list of Internet resources, a list of books for further reading, and an index. A very valuable resource for library collections.

334 *I Am Muslim*
Chalfonte, Jessica.
New York: PowerKids Press, 1996. 24 pp.
ISBN: 0823923754
Grades 1–4
Fundamentals of Islam are introduced through the eyes of a young Muslim child who lives in Detroit. Complemented by color illustrations. "Difficult theological ideas such as salvation are presented in a gentle reassuring manner." — *School Library Journal*

335 *Symbols of Islam*
Chebel, Malek; photographs by Laziz Hamani.
New York: Assouline, 2000. 127 pp.
ISBN: 284323199x
Grades 9–12
This book covers twenty-two very interesting topics regarding doctrines
and rituals in Islam. However, due to its very small print it is not an easy-
to-read book. Includes striking color photographs and a glossary. Transla-
tion of *Symboles de l'Islam.*

336 *Islam and the Muslim Community*
Denny, Fredrick Mathewson.
Prospect Heights, Illinois: Waveland Press, 1998. 137 pp.
ISBN: 1577660072
Grades 11–12
An interpretation of the doctrines and devotional practices is provided by
this author, giving particular attention to their sources in the Qur'an. The
author also examines world events involving Muslims, the Islamic Jihad
movements and the controversy over the adoption of Islamic holy law. The
differences between the Sunni and the Shi'ite forms of Islam, and Islam in
today's world are also discussed. A few black-and-white illustrations, a
glossary and a selected reading list are included.

337 *The Everything Understanding Islam Book: A Complete and Easy to
Read Guide to Muslim Beliefs, Practices, Traditions, and Culture*
Dodge, Christine Huda.
Avon, Massachusetts: Adams Media Corporation, 2003. 289 pp.
ISBN: 1580627838
Grades 7–12
The large print and straightforward explanations makes this book unique
and easy to understand. Discusses all important aspects of Islam, from the
basic beliefs to the Islamic influence on western civilization. Examples are:
the life of Muhammad the Prophet, the Qur'an and Sunnah, the six articles
of faith and other Muslim beliefs, the Five Pillars of Islam, Muslim daily
life, and women in Islam. Dodge is an established author of numerous articles, books, and a newsletter on the subject of Islam. Includes an appendix,
a glossary of Islamic terms, a list of Islamic organizations, and an index.

338 *Allah Gave Me Two Eyes to See*
D'Oyen, Fatima M.; illustrated by Stevan Stratford.

Leicester, England: Islamic Foundation, 1998. 1 v, (unpaged)
ISBN: 0860372839
Grades K–1

A child thinks of all the things he can experience with his five senses. As a result, he should always give thanks to Allah for his many gifts bestowed upon Muslims. Includes beautiful illustrations.

339 *Living Islam*
Egan, Andrew.
Austin, Texas: Raintree Steck-Vaughn Publishers, 2003. 62 pp.
ISBN: 0739863851
Grades 3–6

An extraordinary coverage of the Islamic religion highlighting significant facets students need to be aware of in order to understand Islam. Contains very helpful student guides on each page to emphasize meaningful concepts. Includes color photographs, a glossary, and an index.

340 *The Complete Idiot's Guide to Understanding Islam*
Emerick, Yahiya.
Indianapolis, Indiana: Alpha Books, 2002. 383 pp.
ISBN: 0028642333
Grades 9–12

An outstanding resource written in "plain" English to dispel the popular myths about Muslims and Islam. It is a beginners' guide to the development and history of Islam and Muslim beliefs and their faith. Includes black-and-white pictures, appendices, glossary and an index. Recommended for high school students.

341 *Nadia's Hands*
English, Karen. Illustrated by Jonathan Weiner.
Honesdale, Pennsylvania: Boyds Mills Press, 1999. 32 pp.
ISBN: 1563976676
Grades K–3

Nadia, a Pakistani-American girl, has been chosen to be the flower girl in her aunt's traditional Pakistani wedding. For this festive occasion, Nadia's hands are decorated with elaborate designs using "mehndi" (dye made from the henna tree). After the decoration on her hands is done, Nadia is concerned what her classmates will think since they may not understand that the decoration on her hands is part of her Pakistani culture. It is a cute story accompanied by beautiful color illustrations, and will have a particular appeal for girls. Includes a list of few words in Urdu, the language of Pakistan, with their meanings in English and how to pronounce them. ". . . [G]ives a glimpse into another culture."—*School Library Journal*

342 *Rethinking Islam in the Contemporary World*
Ernst, Carl W.
Edinburgh, Scotland: Edinburgh University Press, 2004. 244 pp.
ISBN: 0748619593
Grades 11–12
Originally published by the University of North Carolina Press under the title *Following Muhammad*, this book provides an analytical view of Islamic religious traditions and the contemporary issues faced by Muslims. The information provides a guide to the fundamental aspects of Islam that includes its sacred sources, ethical systems, and spiritual practices. Includes black-and-white illustrations and an index. Recommended for students with advanced reading skill. ". . . [R]eaders will come away with a good understanding of the different schools of Islamic thought and practice."—*Booklist*

343 *Jamal's Prayer Rug*
Fannoun, Kathy
Chicago: IQRA International Educational Foundation, 1993. 23 pp.
ISBN: 1563163160
Grades K–1
This is a true story of a little Muslim child named Jamal. The Islamic setting and Muslim characters will help children develop a sense of identity. Contains color illustrations. Also includes "Adhan" (call to prayer) with English translation.

344 *Our Loving Grandparents*
Fannoun, Kathy.
Chicago: IQRA International Educational Foundation, 1994. 20 pp.
ISBN: 1563163187
Grades K–1
Every child at a preschool age who has grandparents living very far away will be able to relate to this story. The book emphasizes the bond that grandparents have with their grandchildren. Includes color illustrations.

345 *Understanding Islam: Basic Principles*
Garnet Publishers.

Reading, England: Garnet, 2000. 99 pp.
ISBN: 1859641342
Grades 9–12

Provides information regarding the basic principles of Islam as seen by Muslims themselves in order to facilitate the understanding of Islam by non-Muslims. Frequently asked questions, including those regarding the status of women, are answered as well. Written chiefly in English, with Qur'an selections in English and Arabic. Includes illustrations.

346 *Dinner Time*
Ghazi, Abidullah.
Chicago: IQRA International Educational Foundation, 1992. 24 pp.
ISBN: 1563163012
Grades 2–4

A Muslim family discusses Islamic religious beliefs during dinner time. The emphasis of the conversation is on "praises for Allah" who provides food. Charity to various organizations is also emphasized during the family discussions at the dinner table.

347 *Islam*
Gordon, Mathew S.
New York: Facts on File, 1991. 128 pp.
ISBN: 081602443x
Grades Pre-K–K

This book is a part of "The World Religions" series. It gives a clear and accessible overview of Islamic traditions and institutions. Using a world map, it provides information regarding various regions around the globe where Islam is practiced. In addition, it discusses important rituals and contributions to world civilization. Black-and-white photographs, including maps, complement the text. Includes an index.

348 *Islam*
Gordon, Mathew S.
New York: Facts on File, 2001 (revised edition). 128 pp.
ISBN: 0816044015
Grades 4–7

This revised edition is a comprehensive overview of the impact of Islam historically and in the modern world. The origins of Islam, basic beliefs, structure, places of worship, and rites of passage are discussed as well. A glossary, an index and a list of books for further reading are included.

Black-and-white photos complement the text. Highly recommended by *Booklist* and *RQ*.

349 *Islam: Origins, Practices, Holy Texts, Sacred Persons, Sacred Places*
Gordon, Mathew S.
Oxford, England: Oxford University Press, c2002. 112 pp.
ISBN: 019521885x
Grades 10–12
Various aspects of Islam are presented in this lavishly illustrated volume. Each chapter is followed by a commentary by the author. The views are offered in a very clear and informative manner. Includes an index. "Gordon provides an accessible, well-written and evenhanded introduction to Islam."—*Publishers Weekly*

350 *The Pillars of Islam: An Introduction to the Islamic Faith*
Gumley, Frances and Brian Redhead.
London: BBC Books, 1990. 96 pp.
ISBN: 0563208791
Grades 9–12
Both authors are well-known BBC broadcasters. Unliken other introductory books on Islam, the authors weave stories passed down by oral tradition to explain the basic principles of Islam such as profession of faith, regular prayer, fasting, almsgiving, and pilgrimage. A fascinating approach to the subject. Includes an index. ". . . [E]xcellent introduction for the general reader."—*Library Review*

351 *Islamic Ethics and Personal Conduct*
Hashim, A. S.; reviewed by an imam.
Takoma Park, Maryland: Crescent Publications, 1973, 90 pp.
Grades 6–8
The focus of this book is to emphasize Islamic ethics of personal conduct and dealings on selected subjects. Muslim students would benefit more from this book than non-Muslim students. The text in this book is in English with some Arabic translations.

352 *Islam the Natural Way*
Hashim, Abdul Wahid.
London: Muslim Education and Literary Services, 1989. 195 pp.
ISBN: 0948196092
Grades 9–12

The primary focus of this book is to have an understanding of the main concerns of Islam and of the basic foundation on which the religion was built. The book has been written mainly for the followers of Islam. The layout of the book makes it easy to use and follow. The ten chapters discuss relationships and situations as a Muslim. Includes a very helpful glossary and a list of materials for further reading on the subject.

353 *Muslim Mosque*
Hegedus, Umar.
London: A. & C. Black, 1997. 32 pp.
ISBN: 0713653442
Grades 3–6
Adapted especially for young readers, this lovely book provides an introduction to the understanding of Islam. It answers questions such as, How does someone become a Muslim? What does an Imam do? Why do Muslims face Mecca when they pray? Includes color photographs and an index.

354 *What Muslims Think and How They Live*
Hodges, Rick.
Broomall, Pennsylvania: Mason Crest Publishers, 2004. 112 pp.
ISBN: 1590847024
Grades 9–12
The main purpose of this book is to provide an objective overview of what Muslims believe, how they practice their faith, and the values they consider the most important ones. In 2001–2002, approximately one hundred questions were asked in a survey, conducted by the Gallup Organization, to over 10,000 people in nine predominantly Muslim countries—Iran, Indonesia, Jordan, Kuwait, Lebanon, Morocco, Pakistan, Saudi Arabia, and Turkey, to get their views on culture, family life, politics, religion, and the United States. The results of the survey are analyzed in this book. Includes beautiful color photographs, a chronology, a glossary, a list of Internet resources for additional information, and an index. A very interesting and informative book. Highly recommended for school libraries.

355 *Islam: Opposing Viewpoints*
Hurley, Jennifer A.
San Diego, California: Greenhaven Press, 2001. 170 pp.
ISBN: 0737705140; ISBN (pbk.): 0737705132
Grades 11–12

Experts, policy makers, and concerned citizens discuss their views on Islam in this book. Examples of some of the topics covered are the conflict of values of Islam and the West, the status of women in Islam, Islam and terrorism, and possible U.S. policies toward Islam. Includes an index, a list of organizations to contact, and a glossary. Very informative. ". . . [T]his is a useful, thought-provoking collection that will spark much debate." —*School Library Journal*

356 *What Do We Know about Islam?*
Husain, Shahrukh.
Great Britain: Macdonald Young Books, 1996. 44 pp.
ISBN: 0750027983
Grades 4–7
Beautiful color pictures enhance the explanations about Islam. Basic questions in the who, what, why, when, where, and how formats are answered. The use of the question/answer format creates an interesting approach to the topic. Includes a well-organized glossary and an index. "This title should be a useful addition to other materials on the subject, especially for school reports." —*School Library Journal*

357 *A Brief Illustrated Guide to Understanding Islam*
Ibrahim, I. A.
Houston, Texas: Darussalam, 1997. 74 pp.
ISBN: 9960340112
Grades 11–12
This guide is for non-Muslims who would like to understand Islam. It contains three chapters. The first chapter, "Some Evidence for the Truth of Islam" answers some important questions regarding the Qur'an; the second chapter discusses "Benefits of Islam" and the last chapter provides "General Information on Islam," and corrects misconceptions about Islam. Reviewed and edited by many professors and well-educated people, it is brief and simple to read, is rich in information, and contains references, a list of some Islamic organizations. Color illustrations are included. Truly a wonderful book that should be a part of any library collection. ". . . [A] unique book of dawah, reviewed by a group of specialists to insure correctness and accuracy." —*Al Jumuah Magazine*

358 *Mosques and Minarets*
Ingrams, Doreen. Photography by Alistair Duncan.
St. Paul, Minnesota: EMC Corporation, 1974. 44 pp.

ISBN: 0884361152; ISBN (pbk.): 0884361160
Grades 4–7

Using color illustrations and photographs, this book discusses the basic teachings of Islam and their effect on the different cultures within the Arab world. The first three chapters discuss mainly the founding of Islam, the Qur'an, and the Five Pillars of Islam. The last chapter is devoted to the description and the importance of mosques. It also explains the most striking and often the most attractive feature of a mosque, the minaret, which can be compared to the bell tower of a church. It is an easy-to-read book.

359 *Tell Me about Hajj: What the Hajj Is, Why It's So Important & What It Teaches*
Khan, Saniyasnain.
New Delhi: Goodword Press, 2000. 40 pp.
ISBN: 8187570008
Grades 4–7

Hajj, the sacred pilgrimage to Mecca, is one of the Five Pillars of Islam. Beautifully illustrated in color, the author explains the story of Hajj, which began over 4000 years ago, what the Hajj is, and its importance to Muslims with a special focus on the Prophet Muhammad's Hajj. Over two million believers from around the world gather in Mecca each year for Hajj. The text is presented in a simple and informative manner, enabling young readers to enjoy and understand clearly the meaning of Hajj. Includes "Pilgrims Route" and "Hajj at a Glance" showing various acts and sites of Hajj. In addition, the book contains a glossary of Hajj, a list of places of Hajj, and prayers from the Qur'an and the Hadith with English translation. An excellent book for school libraries.

360 *Maariyah's Day*
Kibria, Shaila.
Annandale, Virginia: Trancom International, 2000. 40 pp.
ISBN: 1893538001
Grades 2–5

Reading this book will allow young children to understand significant multicultural and Islamic issues, helping those who may suffer from religious intolerance to better understand the significance of certain traditions, practices, and clothing in Islam. Color illustrations make the book very interesting. Highly recommended for any parent and teachers of young children.

361 *What Should We Say?: A Selection of Prayers for Daily Use*
Kidwai, A. R. and F. M. D'Oyen; illustrations by Stevan Stratford.
Leicester, England: Islamic Foundation, 1999. 35 pp.
ISBN: 0860372677
Grades 3–5

A useful tool of the translation of Arabic daily prayers used by children as well as adults. Includes an excellent explanation of the meanings of the individual prayers. Also includes color illustrations, a glossary and a transliteration of English/Arabic alphabet. Appropriate for Muslim children.

362 *Islam*
Knight, Khadijah.
New York: Thomson Learning, 1995. 48 pp.
ISBN: 1568473788
Grades 4–6

Through colorful photographs and a fascinating narrative, the author discusses the origins, the traditions, and the beliefs of Islam. The author, an educator in England, is involved with the needs of young Muslims in all areas of education. In this book, she explains home and family life in African-American Muslim communities, post-communist Eastern Europe, and Russia. Includes key dates in the history of Islam, the Islamic calendar, a glossary, and an index. A very interesting book.

363 *Understanding Islam: An Introduction to the Muslim World*
Lippman, Thomas W.
New York: Meridian, 1995. 198 pp.
ISBN: 0452011604
Grades 11–12

The author, who served in Cairo as the *Washington Post* Bureau chief for the Middle East for over three years, provides an informative and insightful introduction to Islam both as a religion and as a political-economic force. In addition to discussing the life of the Prophet Muhammad and the Five Pillars of Islam, he explains the differences that divide Islam, the influence of Islam on world affairs, today's Islamic community, the Gulf War, and the internal politics of Egypt, Syria, Pakistan, and other Islamic nations. Includes a bibliography, a glossary, and an index.

364 *Teen Life in the Middle East*
Mahdi, Ali Akbar.
Westport, Connecticut: Greenwood Press, 2003. 268 pp.

ISBN: 031331893X
Grades 9–12

This unique book, containing black-and-white photographs, offers insight into the typical day, interests, social, and cultural lives of teens from Iran, Iraq, Israel, Jordan, Kuwait, Lebanon, Palestinian territories, Saudi Arabia, Syria, Turkey, United Arab Emirates, and Yemen. In addition to providing teen readers in the West an understanding of the lives of their counterparts in the Middle East, this volume also discusses the similarities and the differences between them. Each chapter is followed by a resource guide, a list of websites, and pen pal/chat. It is a very timely resource that is highly recommended for school libraries. "This is a unique and interesting resource that helps describe the cultures of the various countries in terms that are relevant to young people." — *School Library Journal*

365 *Islam*
Maqsood, Ruqaiyyah Waris.
Chicago:,Contemporary Books, 2003. 263 pp.
ISBN: 0071419632
Grades 8–12

This comprehensive guide to the world's second largest faith covers all aspects of Islam. Makes a clear distinction between Islam itself as revealed in the Qur'an, the teachings and the way of life of the Prophet, and various social and cultural aspects of Islamic society. Includes an index, glossary and illustrations.

366 *Islam*
Morris, Neil.
Columbus, Ohio: Peter Bedrick Books, 2002. 46 pp.
ISBN: 0872266931
Grades 4–7

Beautifully illustrated in color, this book covers the origins of Islam, the life of the Prophet Muhammad, the basic teachings of Islam, worship, Islamic festivals, Islamic art, women in Islam, and Islam in Asia and in Africa. Includes a very helpful glossary and an index.

367 *A Day in the Life of a Muslim Child*
Mujahid, Abdul Malik. Translated by Tariq Alvi and Anjum-Alvi.
Riyadh, Saudi Arabia: Darussalam, 1997. 64 pp.
ISBN: 9960717453
Grades 2–5

Describes rituals and practices of a Muslim boy. The prayers used in daily activities throughout the day provide an understanding of the relationship of religion and daily activities. Includes color photographs.

368 *Islam*
Penney, Sue.
Austin, Texas: Raintree Steck-Vaughn, 1997. 48 pp.
ISBN: 0817243941
Grades 4–6

The origins, evolution, teachings, and celebrations of Islam are discussed in this book. Outstanding and clearly organized, this is an easy-to-read book. Includes an index, color photographs, maps, and graphs.

369 *Mecca*
Ross, Mandy.
Chicago: Raintree, 2003. 32 pp.
ISBN: 0739860801
Grades 2–5

Color photographs enhance the text in this informative book about Mecca and the beliefs and practices followed by Muslims. The author explains why Mecca is so special to people of Muslim faith, and investigates the rich religion, culture, festivals, and history associated with the site. It also includes is information about two additional Islamic holy cities, namely Medina and Jerusalem. In addition to the stunning photography and clear explanatory text, the book includes box features that expand on issues discussed in the text. A glossary and an index are included. "Boxed insets make the format exceptionally attractive." —*Booklist*

370 *Islam in the World*
Ruthven, Malise.
New York: Oxford University Press, c2000. 472pp.
ISBN: 0195138414
Grades 11–12

The author provides an essential summary of Islam in this second revised edition. A full overview of Islam in its historical, geographical, and social settings is presented by the author. The book covers pilgrimage to Mecca, Muhammad and the Qur'an, the development of divine law, the mystic tradition, and various Islamic sects. In addition, this book also features a chapter that discusses women in Islam, the challenges faced in Islam in today's climate of globalization, and the Taliban movement in Afghanistan. Includes bibliographical references, maps, and an index.

371 *Islam: A Primer*
Sabini, John.
Washington, D.C.: Middle East Editorial Associates, 1990. 122 pp.
ISBN: 0918992087
Grades 10–12
   Written in a clear manner, this book introduces a reader to the history, beliefs and practices, civilization and culture of Islam. The author has listed
and defined key terms and some famous people used in the text. Terms that
are useful in understanding particular aspects of Islam are also listed in the
glossary. Includes "Suggestions for Further Reading" and maps. It is a very
useful resource for a general reader who is interested in learning various aspects of Islam.

372 *Islam: A Concise Introduction*
Smith, Huston.
San Francisco, California: HarperSanFrancisco, 2001. 100 pp.
ISBN: 0060095571
Grades 9–12
   This book offers a revealing look into the heart of a tradition with more
than one billion adherents worldwide. It addresses issues such as the true
meaning of Jihad, women's role in Islamic societies, and the remarkable
growth of Islam in America.

373 *The Muslim World*
Tames, Richard.
Morristown, New Jersey: Silver Burdett Co., 1982. 45 pp.
ISBN: 0382067193
Grades 6–9
   A beautiful book that explores what it means to be a Muslim. It explores
the history, principles, and customs of Islam including the significance of
the Five Pillars of Islam as well as the efforts of Islamic countries to remain
traditional in a modern world. Supplemented by color photographs, this
book includes a Muslim calendar, a glossary, a list of books for further
reading, places to visit, helpful organizations, and an index. A great addition to any library.

374 *Islam: The Basics*
Whitehead, Kim.
Broomall, Pennsylvania: Mason Crest Publishers, 2004. 112 pp.
ISBN: 1590846974
Grades 10–12

This is one of the four volumes titled "Introducing Islam." Illustrated with color photographs, this book is an excellent overview of Muslim beliefs and values and their practice of Islam in their everyday lives. The book provides the historical background of Islam's emergence on the Arabian Peninsula during the seventh century, and explores the spread of Islam throughout the world during the centuries that followed. In addition, it also discusses major Islamic sects, Islamic laws, celebrations and festivals. The last chapter discusses crucial issues that are currently faced by Muslims. Includes a chronology, Internet resources, suggestions for "Further Reading," and an index. Color map and photographs enhance the text. An excellent resource.

375 *Islam*
Wilkinson, Philip; Batul Salazar.
New York: Dorling Kindersley, 2002. 64 pp.
ISBN: 0789488701; ISBN (pbk.): 078948871x
Grades 4–6
Every page has beautiful color photographs and illustrations to enhance the information that helps the reader discover the faith, culture, and history that have shaped the modern Islamic world. Includes an index. A wonderful asset for any library. ". . . [S]tunning in-depth look at the complex world of one of the world's great religions."—*Publishers Weekly*

376 *Muslim Mosque*
Wood, Angela.
Milwaukee, Wisconsin: Gareth Stevens Publishing, 2000. 32 pp.
ISBN: 0836826094
Grades 1–4
Beautifully enhanced by color pictures, this book describes what happens inside a mosque and introduces the Muslim faith. The words are in a large print which makes it an easy-to-read book. Includes color pictures and photographs, glossary, bibliographical references and an index.

QUR'AN

377 *The Quran in Plain English*
Leicester, England: The Islamic Foundation, 1993. 236 pp.
Grades 7–12

A very useful resource, particularly for children and young people, to gain understanding of God's final message for all times and all places, revealed to the Prophet Muhammad. Written in simple English and supplemented with several explanatory notes and a glossary, this book will help readers to understand the meaning and message of the Qur'an. It is well organized in that each "surah" (verse) is accompanied by English translation. Includes Arabic names and their common English equivalents, a glossary of Arabic terms, a select bibliography, and an index. Well recommended.

378 *Glimpses of the Holy Qur'an*
Azizullah, Muhammad.
Karachi: The World Federation of Islamic Missions, 1963. 96 pp.
Grades 7–10
   The main topics covered in this book are: what the Qur'an is; oneness of God; missions of all important Prophets; judgments, rewards, and punishments; and prohibitions ordained by the Holy Qur'an. Although the map included in this book is outdated, the text can be very useful to those who want to know the basics about the Holy Qur'an. Each verse in Arabic is followed by the English translation and interpretation. The book is easy to understand. Muslim children would benefit from this the most.

379 *The Qur'an and Islam*
Ganeri, Anita; illustrations by Tracy Fennell.
Mankato, Minnesota: Smart Apple Media, 2004. 30 pp.
ISBN: 1583402411
Grades 4–6
   This book is one of the "Sacred Texts" series written by Anita Ganeri. The author explains the history and practices of the religion of Islam, especially as revealed through the sacred book, the Qur'an. It discusses how Muslims incorporate the text from the Qur'an in their daily lives and worship. Muslims believe that Allah revealed His wishes for the world to a man called the Prophet Muhammad. Since the Prophet could not write, the messages were written by his followers. Includes color photographs, illustrations, a glossary, and an index. It is a must for a middle school library. "Students will find a wealth of information for reports, much of which can't easily be found in other series for this age group."—*Booklist*

380 *Al-Khidr, the Green One: At the Place Where the Two Seas Meet and the Hidden Treasure of the Mercy of Allah*
Halman, Hugh Talat.

Skokie, Illinois: IQRA International Education Foundation, 2000. 34 pp.
Grades 4–7

This is the story of al-Khidr (the Green One) and of Moses, a Prophet and Messenger of God. Moses is guided by Al-Khidr in discovering the deepest truth of the Mercy of God. The account in this book is based on the narrative in The Sacred Qur'an. Includes color pictures.

381 *Miracles of the Qur'an*
Yahya, Harun.
Ontario, Canada: Al-Attique Publishers Inc., 2001. 99 pp.
ISBN: 1894264533
Grades 6–12

A fascinating book that discusses the matchless style of the Qur'an and the superior wisdom in it. The author states that "the Qur'an has many miraculous attributes proving that it is a revelation from God. One of these attributes is the fact that a number of scientific truths that we have only been able to uncover by the technology of the twentieth century were stated in the Qur'an 1,400 years ago." These statements are supported by many scientific facts, expressed in the verses of the Qur'an. Some of the examples are: the origin and expansion of the universe, orbits, the roundness of the earth, the function of mountains, the identity in the fingerprint, and several more. In addition to the scientific miracles of the Qur'an, messages regarding the future and the historical miracles of the Qur'an are presented in this book. Includes beautiful color photographs.

11

Major Contributions

One will find in this chapter eight resources that provide information regarding the discoveries attributed to scientists and scholars after the birth of the Prophet Muhammad in 570 AD, and their effect on Western civilization in the centuries to follow. Out of these eight resources, six are for the high school, and two for the elementary school grade levels. There was a scarcity of resources for middle school grade level.

382 *Science in Early Islamic Cultures*
Beshore, George.
New York: Franklin Watts, 2000.
ISBN: 0531159175
Grades 4–8
   The extraordinary scientific discoveries and advancements in the Islamic world after the birth of the Prophet Muhammad in 570 AD, and their effect on Western civilization in the centuries to follow are discussed in this volume. Includes color and black-and-white illustrations, glossary, index, and very helpful resources are included.

383 *Islamic Technology: An Illustrated History*
Hasan, Ahmad Yusuf; Donald Routledge Hill.
Cambridge University Press [with] Unesco, 1992. 304 pp.
ISBN: 0521422396
Grades 11–12
   Upon request by UNESCO, the authors sought to put together the story of Islamic technology. Although readers in an honors class would find this book very interesting, readers lacking a strong science background would

find it too complicated. Includes black-and-white illustrations, pictures, drawings, and an index. "Lavishly illustrated, this book explores the major technological achievements of Islamic civilizations."—*Editorial Review*

384 *The House of Wisdom*
Heide, Florence Parry and Judith Heide Gilliland; illustrated by Mary GrandPre.
New York: DK Ink, 1999. [36] pp.
ISBN: 0789425629
Grades 4–6

   This is the story of Ishaq, the son of Hunayn, a translator to the Caliph of ancient Baghdad during the ninth century. Ishaq travels the world in search of precious books and manuscripts and brings them back to the House of Wisdom. The House of Wisdom was a learning institution and a library, where scholars preserved the great contributions of the ancient world to medicine, astronomy, philosophy, history, geography, and mathematics. Thousands of scholars from all over the world came to the House of Wisdom to read, to exchange ideas, and to translate the dusty manuscripts that came to them by camel and by sea. Through their work, Caliph al-Ma'mun, Hunayn, and Ishaq played important parts in this period of enlightenment, and contributed toward the civilization for the rest of the world. In illustrating this book, Mary Grandpre, who was inspired by the richly patterned Islamic art and structured "the book's pages with framed boxes and borders reminiscent of old Islamic books" made a significant contribution. Includes a map. A very interesting resource.

385 *The Archaeology of Islam*
Insoll, Timothy.
Malden, Massachusetts: Blackwell Publishers, Inc., 1999. 274 pp.
ISBN: 0631201149; ISBN (pbk.): 0631201157
Grades 11–12

   The author examines the archaeological effect of Islam on all aspects of life. The distinct presence of Muslim life is evident in the archaeological records. Includes black-and-white photographs, maps, references, and index.

386 *The World of Islamic Civilization*
Le Bon, Gustave; translated by David Macrae.
New York: Tudor Publishing Company, 1974. 141 pp.
Grades 11–12

The first three chapters in this book cover the traditional lifestyle of Islam, Muslim institutions, and the Muslim religion. The chapters that follow discuss how the influence of the Arabs throughout the Middle East was felt not only in religion, language, and the arts, but also in sciences. The last chapter discusses the impact that the Arabs had on the West through science and literature. Includes some color, but mostly black-and-white illustrations. An index would have been helpful.

387 *The Arabs in the Golden Age*
Moktefi, Mokhtar.
Brookfield, Connecticut: Millbrook Press, 1992. 64 pp.
ISBN: 1590847008
Grades 11–12

Who are the Arabs? What is the relationship between the Arabs and the Muslim religion? There is a lack of understanding about the Arab world in the West today. The author provides an informative overview of the period when the Arabs spread their religion, art, architecture, calligraphy, technology, and great knowledge of the ancient world throughout the Middle East and North Africa. Attractive color illustrations and maps complement the text. Includes "Dates to Remember," a glossary, and an index. An excellent resource.

388 *Introduction to Islamic Civilisation*
Savory, R. M., editor.
Cambridge, England: Cambridge University Press, 1976. 204 pp.
ISBN: 9521207770; ISBN (pbk.): 052109948x
Grades 11–12

The introductory chapter discusses the geographical, ethnic, and linguistic background of the Middle East. After a brief history of the Islamic period, the book covers the religious, philosophical, and legal foundations of Islamic society and its contributions to world civilization in the fields of literature, art, science, and medicine. The time-scale covers the pre-Islamic, medieval, and modern periods until the early 1970s. This book is based on a series of adult-education programs broadcast on Canadian radio, organized by members of the Department of Islamic Studies at the University of Toronto. Includes black-and-white illustrations, "A Suggested Background Reading," a glossary and an index. The impact of these illustrations would have been more powerful if the illustrations were in color. Contains a very detailed account of the subject that should be very appealing to researchers who want to learn about Islamic civilization in various fields.

389 *A Muslim Primer: Beginner's Guide to Islam*
Zepp, Ira G.; illustrated by Jody Kathryn Zepp.
Westminster, Maryland: Wakefield Editions, 1992. 292 pp.
ISBN: 0870611887
Grades 9–12

A very informative and helpful book, particularly to those who need introduction to the basic truths about Islam. In addition to topics such as beliefs of Islam, message of the Qur'an, ethics, Five Pillars of Islam, and the status of women, the author has included a chapter which highlights some very important contributions from the Middle East in art, architecture, sciences, literature, etc. during the Golden Age of Islam. Well researched, illustrated in black-and-white, it is an easy book to understand. Highly recommended for high school libraries. "Superb introduction to Islam for the non-Islamic reader."—*Library Journal*

12

Muslims in the West

This chapter provides thirteen resources relevant to Muslims who have set-tled in Western countries and the challenges they face. There are eight for the high school, one for the middle school, and four for the elementary school grade levels.

390 *The American Encounter with Islam*
Anjum, Mir.
Broomall, Pennsylvania: Mason Crest Publishers, 2004. 128 pp.
ISBN: 1590846990
Grades 10–12

An in-depth and multifaceted view of the Muslim experience in the United States is depicted in this well-written book. A summary of the basic teachings of Islam and the history of American Muslims from the era of slavery to the Muslim immigration to converts is discussed. The present and future of the American Muslim community is also examined. The text is enhanced by color photographs. It is a wonderful book that contains a chronology, a glossary, Internet resources, and an index.

391 *Unveiling Islam: An Insider's Look at Muslim Life and Beliefs*
Caner, Erjun Mehmet and Emir Fethi Caner.
Grand Rapids, Michigan: Kregel Publications, 2002. 251 pp.
ISBN: 0825424003
Grades 9–12

Written by two brothers who were raised as Sunni Muslims but are now prominent Christian theology professors, this book presents a view of the scope of Muslim practices, ethics, and beliefs, including the main differences between Christian and Islamic beliefs. A national best seller with an emphasis on Christianity, it includes a glossary of Arabic Islamic terms. A highly recommended resource.

392 *American Muslims: The New Generation*
Hasan, Asma Gull.
New York: Continuum, 2002. 204 pp.
ISBN: 0826414168
Grades 11–12
Exceptionally well-written by a self-described Muslim woman, Asma Hasan, this book will help Americans understand anti-Muslim stereotypes and learn more about Islam, the fastest growing religion in America. The author also expresses her views regarding the American-born children of immigrants and their future when it comes to adapting their faith to American culture. It includes an index and a study guide. A very highly recommended book for Muslims as well as non-Muslims.

393 *Bad Day Good Day*
Hutchinson, Uthman; illustrated by Abdulmuttalib Fahema.
Beltsville, Maryland: Amana Publications, 1995. 17 pp.
ISBN: 0915957477
Grades 1–2
The story centers around an American Muslim family living in a small city in the United States. The characters of the story represent the parents, their three school-aged children, and their relatives and friends from Afghanistan, America, Malaysia, and Pakistan.

394 *Understanding Your Muslim Neighbour*
Iqbal, Muhammad and Maryam K. Iqbal.
Guildford and London: Lutterworth Press, 1976. 45 pp.
ISBN: 0718818571
Grades 4–7
This is a story about Bashir, a six-year-old, and his ten-year-old sister, Shamim, who moved from their Muslim village in Pakistan to England to join their father. While practicing their own religion, Islam, the children had to make adjustments by learning some of the traditions, festivals, and customs practiced by people in the Western culture. Includes black-and-white photographs.

395 *Neighbors: Muslims in North America*
Mallon, Elias D.

New York: Friendship Press, 1989. 104 pp.
ISBN: 0377001988
Grades 10–12

Stereotype images about Muslims and the religion of Islam exist among some non-Muslims. The author attempts to help readers create positive image of Islam and Muslims in the eyes of the westerners by introducing them to "the Muslim next door." He believes that prejudices begin to break down when a person begins to realize that not everyone in a group fits that image, and that "prejudices break down further when a person becomes a good neighbor or a friend to someone who belongs to a minority group that suffers from 'bad press' or prejudice." Nine men and women of different ages and ethnic and educational backgrounds are interviewed by the author, who hopes that reading this book will allow the reader to feel more comfortable about getting to know the Muslim who works as his or her colleague or who lives in his or her neighborhood. A very helpful book for those adults who are prejudiced against Muslims and Islam, and wish to have a better understanding regarding Muslims and Islam. The book uses a question-and-answer format, and is quite interesting and easy to read. Recommended for non-Muslim families.

396 *A Young Muslim's Guide to the Modern World*
Nasr, Seyyed Hossein.
Chicago: Kazi Publications, 1994. 270 pp.
ISBN: 1567444768
Grades 11–12

An instructive text for Muslim youth wishing to practice Islam in a Western environment. The author's focus is to have young Muslims become familiar with their cultural roots, to have an understanding of their religion, and to gain familiarity with the modern world from the Islamic point of view. Well-written, this book addresses primarily Muslim youth who are confronting various facets of the modern world through their educational and social experiences and not the established scholars of Islam. Includes an index. "First of its kind in any language, presents eternal truths of Islam as well as Western religious and intellectual tradition as they confront each other." — Robert Siegel of NPR's *All Things Considered*.

397 *Islam in the United States of America*
Nyang, Sulayman S.
Chicago: ABC International Group, Inc. 1999. 165 pp.

ISBN: 1871031699
Grades 11–12

A fascinating collection of essays written by an expert on Islamic studies. Professor Sulayman Nyang reveals his insights and research findings on the emerging Muslim community in the United States. This book is essential to understand the issues relevant to religious plurality and multiculturalism in American society. Includes a bibliography and an index. Extremely informative and enlightening; however, only a few chapters which pertain to the subject would be of specific interest to readers of this book.

398 *Muslims and the West*
Sears, Evelyn.
Broomall, Pennsylvania: Mason Crest Publishers, 2004. 112 pp.
ISBN: 1590847008
Grades 6–9

This well-researched and clearly written book examines the history of interaction between Muslims and the West in the fourteen centuries since the birth of Islam. The spread of Islamic influence into western Europe, the impact of the crusades, the legacy of European colonialism, and the United States's role in Muslim lands during the past fifty years is also explored. Includes a chronology, a glossary, a list of Internet and other resources, an index, and very effective color photographs and maps. Highly recommended for library collections.

399 *The Arab Americans*
Temple, Bob.
Philadelphia, Pennsylvania: Mason Crest Publishers, 2003. 64 pp.
ISBN: 1590841026
Grades 4–7

A history of Arab immigration to the United States and Canada, from the nineteenth century to the present day, due to religious strife in the Middle East, political turmoil, and poor economic conditions, is presented. Many Arab Americans have found North America to be a place where they can be successful and earn a profitable living for themselves and their families. Arab Americans' lives after the 9/11 terrorist attack are also discussed. According to this book, Arab Americans will continue to be a vital part of America's melting pot in the future. Includes a very useful chronology, names of famous Arab Americans in various fields, a glossary, a list of books for further reading, Internet resources and an index are included. The color photographs complement the text. Very nicely organized and interesting, this book is highly recommended for school libraries.

400 *Coming to America: A Muslim Family's Story*
Wolf, Bernard.
New York: Lee & Low Books, 2003. [46] pp.
ISBN: 1584300868
Grades 2–5

This is a story of a Muslim family from Alexandria, Egypt, who moved to New York City to have a better life for themselves. Like many other immigrant families, this family experiences joys and hardships during the transition to American life. With the help of captivating photographs, the author also discusses Muslim festivals and traditions.

401 *American Islam: Growing Up Muslim in America*
Wormser, Richard.
New York: Walker and Co., 2002. 130 pp.
ISBN: 0802776280
Grades 7–12

The author provides information regarding the growing population of Muslims in the United States. Some of the topics covered are: historical overview of Islam, love and marriage, dealing with peer pressure, and adaptation of ancient customs to modern life. Includes black-and-white illustrations. Should appeal to teenagers.

402 *Discovering Islam: And Muslims of the United States*
Yousef, Ahmed, and Imam Fawaz Damra, compilers.
Annandale, Virginia: United Association for Studies and Research, 2002.
    26 pp.
Grades 8–12

Although covering only 26 pages, this book presents a wealth of basic information on a religion that is often misunderstood in the United States. In the aftermath of the September 11th attacks, due to ignorance many hate crimes were committed against American Muslims, or people who "looked" Muslim. This publication clarifies some of the misunderstanding and ignorance regarding the second largest religion in America. Reading this simple book will allow one to understand many of the traditional values, customs, and practices of Islam. Topics such as the Five Pillars of Islam, contributions of Muslims to Western civilization, women in Islam, a brief history of Islam in the United States, distribution of the Muslim population in the world, and Islam in the eyes of the West are addressed. A section on "Frequently Asked Questions" is a great inclusion that addresses many basic common questions. Color illustrations are very effective. In addition, the book also lists "Useful Resources for Further Reading." An excellent book for anyone who wishes to learn about Islam by reading just twenty-six pages. Highly recommended for parents, teachers, and librarians.

13

Nation of Islam

The reader will find resources related to the historical rise of the Black Muslims and some of the most prominent leaders of the Nation of Islam. This chapter contains seven resources; one for the high school, one for the middle school, and five for the elementary school grade levels.

403 *The Black Muslims*
Banks, William.
Philadelphia, Pennsylvania: Chelsea House Publishers, 1997. 124 pp.
ISBN: 0791025934
Grades 5–10
   Presents the history of the rise of various black movements including the Nation of Islam. The book helps to understand the racial injustice and economic hardships faced by African Americans. It has some interesting information; however, it lacks a smooth transition from one movement to another. The chronology is an excellent overview of the rise of Black Muslims in the United States. Includes black-and-white photographs, and a list of books for further reading. "A well-written overview that covers the early founders and dissension within the Nation of Islam." —*School Library Journal*

404 *Malcolm X*
Benson, Michael.
Minneapolis, Minnesota: Lerner Publications, 2002. 112 pp.
ISBN: 0822550253
Grades 5–8
   This is a very interesting story about one of the most influential and dedicated African American leaders of the 1950s and 1960s, Malcolm X, the

leading spokesman for the Nation of Islam. He traveled to Mecca and Saudi Arabia to learn more about Islam. His early life of crime through his violent assassination is described in this book. Includes black-and-white illustrations, a selected bibliography, and an index. "A readable biography that presents a balanced account of this influential but controversial African-American leader." — *School Library*

405 *Muhammad Ali*
Buckley, James.
Milwaukee, Wisconsin: World Almanac Library, 2004. 48 pp.
ISBN: 0836850963; ISBN (pbk.): 0836852567
Grades 4–6

A convert to the Nation of Islam in 1964, Muhammad Ali (alias Cassius Clay) is considered to be one of the greatest boxers of all time. The South was still segregated when he was born on January 17, 1942, in Louisville, Kentucky. Ali learned that fame did not open doors to end segregation. He rose to prominence during the Civil Rights Movement in the 1960s. He was as famous for his controversial words and actions as he was for boxing skills. Popular around the world, he is a man who believed in himself and stuck to his principles. Includes color photographs, time line, a glossary, Internet sites, and an index.

406 *Louis Farrakhan*
Deangelis, Therese.
Philadelphia, Pennsylvania: Chelsea House Publishers, 1998. 112 pp.
ISBN: 0791046885; ISBN (pbk.): 0791046893
Grades 6–12

A well-written biography of the African-American who at one time dreamed of a career as a violinist before he joined the Nation of Islam, rose in its ranks, and eventually became its leader. This book also examines the major leaders of the Nation of Islam. The emergence of Louis Farrakhan as a prominent and powerful voice in the African-American community is well documented by the author. Includes black-and-white photographs, a chronology, a list of "Black Americans of Achievement," a list of books for "Further Reading" and an index.

407 *Malcolm X: A Voice for Black America*
Diamond, Arthur.
Hillside, New Jersey: Enslow Publishers, 1994. 128 pp.

ISBN: 0894904353

Grades 4–6

The author explores the multi-faceted life of one of the most controversial and influential African-American Muslim leaders. The book describes his troubled childhood, his years as a national leader in the Nation of Islam, and his assassination. Includes black-and-white illustrations, a chronology, a list of additional resources, and an index.

408 *Louis Farrakhan and the Nation of Islam*

Haskins, James.

New York: Walker and Co., 1996. 152 pp.

ISBN: 0802784224; ISBN (pbk.): 0802784232

Grades 5–8

The author crafts a biography of Louis Farrakhan, an African American who dreamed of a career as a violinist before he joined the Nation of Islam and became its leader. Haskins also discusses Farrakhan's role as the organizer of the Million Man March, his relationship with Malcolm X, his alliance with Jesse Jackson, and the assassination plot against him. The book contains critical material to understand the racial injustice and economic hardships faced by African Americans. This book includes a helpful index and some black-and-white illustrations. "Haskin's book is more of an account of the birth of the Nation of Islam than a biography of Farrakhan."
—*School Library Journal*

409 *Malcolm X: A Fire Burning Brightly*

Meyers, Walter Dean.

New York: HarperCollins Publishers, 2000. [33] pp.

ISBN: 0060277076. (Pbk.) ISBN: 006442118X

Grades 3–5

Written by an award-winning writer of fiction, nonfiction, and poetry for young people, and a five-time winner of the Coretta Scott King Award, this is an excellent book about the life of Malcolm X, one of the most controversial and misunderstood men of the twentieth century. A chronology of events in Malcolm's life and color illustrations are included. "A compelling account. . . . A perfect blend of well-written text and well-executed illustrations."—*School Library Journal* "Myers makes the complexities of Malcolm X's story accessible without compromising its integrity."—*The Horn Book*

14

Resistance versus Terrorism

This chapter provides eighteen resources regarding the tragic attacks of September 11, 2001, in the United States, including the differences between radical Islamic fundamentalists and other Muslims. There are seven resources for the high school, four for the middle school, and seven for the elementary school grade levels.

410 *World Book Focus on Terrorism*
Chicago: World Book, 2003. 160 pp.
ISBN: 071661295x
Grades 8–12
  Who were the hijackers who attacked the United States on September 11, 2001? Why did they act the way they did? What weapons and methods do terrorists use? How does the government fight terrorism? Many questions such as these and more are answered in this book. Divided into seven sections. The introductory section discusses the 9/11 terrorist attack. The next six sections discuss the Arab-Israeli conflict, the Middle East and surrounding areas, conflicts within Islam, methods and weapons used by terrorists, homeland security, and past and present terrorism. Includes very effective maps and illustrations—some are in color and others are in black and white. Additional resources and websites are provided throughout the book. Also includes an index. It is an excellent resource that covers many important topics pertaining to the subject of terrorism. However, the print is rather small, which makes it difficult to read.

411 *The Place of Tolerance in Islam*
Abou El Fadi, Khaled; edited by Joshua Cohen and Ian Lague.

Boston: Beacon Press, 2002. 117 pp.
ISBN: 0807002291
Grades 11–12

The author, Abou El Fadi, a well-known critic of Islamic Puritanism, argues that Islam is a deeply tolerant religion. Violence against nonbelievers arises from misreading of the Qur'an, including Jihad, or so-called Holy War. He also claims that there is no such basis in Muslim theology, but instead, intolerance has grown out of social and political conflict. This book should help to clarify some of the misconceptions regarding the Islamic beliefs and values.

412 *Blood from Stones: The Secret Financial Network of Terror*
Farah, Douglas.
New York: Broadway Books, 2004. 225 pp.
ISBN: 0767915623
Grades 11–12

Since January 2004, Douglas Farah, the award-winning member of the investigative staff and a foreign correspondent for the *Washington Post* and other publications, has worked as a consultant and a senior fellow at the National Strategy Information Center. It was during the time when he was the *Washington Post*'s West African Bureau chief after 9/11 that he uncovered indisputable evidence that terrorist groups were laundering their cash by trading it for diamonds mined in Sierra Leone and Liberia. This is truly an intriguing account of corrupt African officials, members of Al Qaeda and Hezbollah, arms dealers, Arabs in the United States and around the world who created the financial support to promote terrorism. Young men particularly would find this subject interesting. It reads like a series of espionage plots.

413 *America's War in Afghanistan*
Fiscus, James W.
New York: Rosen Publishing Group, 2004. 64 pp.
ISBN: 0823945529
Grades 5–8

Part of the series titled "War and Conflict in the Middle East," this book discusses the war between the United States and Afghanistan after the September 11 attack on the World Trade Center in New York City, the Pentagon near Washington, D.C., and a farm field in Pennsylvania. The attacks of September 11 were tied to a radical Islamic group, Al Qaeda, which was based in Afghanistan. The author provides a very useful historical background for the rise of Al Qaeda and the Taliban, allies of Al Qaeda. Includes color photographs, a map, additional sources for more information on this subject, a glossary, and an index.

414 *Understanding September 11th: Answering Questions about the Attacks on America*
Frank, Mitch.
New York: Viking, 2002. 136 pp.
ISBN: 0670035823; ISBN (pbk.): 0670035874
Grades 7–12

The author provides an outstanding, straightforward explanation of the historical and religious issues that resulted in the 9/11 terrorist attack on America. The *Time* magazine reporter answers the questions, Who were the hijackers? What is terrorism? Why did the terrorists target the United States? Who are the Taliban? Who is Osama bin Laden? The book also covers invaluable information regarding the Middle East. Includes black-and-white photographs, biographical references, and an index. Highly recommended resource. "He presents an empathetic picture of Middle Eastern resentments. He (the author) is blunt in laying out the religious, political, and economic reasons for the U.S. interest in the region and passionate about civil liberties."— *School Library Journal*

415 *The Attack on the Pentagon on September 11, 2001*
Gard, Carolyn
New York: The Rosen Publishing Group, 2003. 64 pp.
ISBN: 0823938581
Grades 4–6

This is an excellent historical reference book about the 9/11 attack by terrorists on the Pentagon. It helps one to understand the people and events leading up to the 9/11 attack. Includes an index, a bibliography, and a list of some very useful resources for further reading. Color photographs are very helpful. A very good resource in a school library collection.

416 *Islamic Fundamentalism*
Gunderson, Cory Gideon.
Edina, Minnesota: ABDO & Daughters, 2004. 48 pp.
ISBN: 1591974119
Grades 4–9

This is an overview of the differences between radical Islamic fundamentalists and other Muslims. As part of the series titled "World in Conflict, the Middle East," the book discusses the Five Pillars of Islam, Islam and the West, acts of terror on September 11, hijacking, kidnapping, hostage taking, and the outcomes of Islamic fundamentalism.

417 *September 11, 2001: Attack on New York City*
Hampton, Wilborn.
Cambridge, Massachusetts: Candlewick Press, 2003. 145 pp.
ISBN: 0763619493
Grades 6–9
The tragic attacks in the United States on September 11, 2001, are described in a very clear and organized manner. Nearly 3,000 people were killed at the World Trade Center. The story of what happened in New York on that sad day is shared firsthand by several people who lived through it. Many journalists covered the events of September 11, and their accounts provide information about the firefighters, the attack on the Pentagon, and the crash in Pennsylvania. Includes black-and-white photographs, a bibliography, and an index. A very valuable resource for teachers and parents, for explaining the tragic day. "There are many, perhaps too many books about 9/11 written for young people, but this is one of the best."—*Booklist*

418 *Jihad: Islamic Fundamentalist Terrorism*
Katz, Samuel M.
Minneapolis, Minnesota: Lerner Publications Co., 2004. 72 pp.
ISBN: 0822540312
Grades 7–12
For centuries, misunderstanding, hatred, and fear have fostered fundamentalist terrorist groups to expel Western governments from the Islamic world. The author, a renowned terrorism expert, provides readers of this book a comprehensive study of the key elements involved in such movements in the world. The author discusses the history, important conflicts, and ideals of major fundamentalist Islamic terrorist groups, including Al Qaeda, al-Jihad warriors in Egypt, Hezbollah in Lebanon, Armed Islamic Group in Algeria, and others. Includes black-and-white photographs, maps, a selected bibliography, a timeline, websites for additional information, and an index. A very useful resource for those who want to learn about this subject. "Katz explains extremely complicated history and issues clearly and concisely and in adequate depth."—*Booklist*

419 *9.11.01: Terrorists Attack the U.S.*
Lalley, Pat.
Austin, Texas: Raintree Steck-Vaughn Publishers, 2002. 48 pp.

ISBN: 0739860216
Grades 4–8

The September 11, 2001, terrorist attack on the World Trade Center and the Pentagon—the first significant act of war by a foreign enemy on the U.S. mainland in almost two centuries, is explained in the introductory chapter. First-person accounts by several individuals who were affected by the 9/11 attack shed light on the events of that day. The background information on Islam, the history of the Middle East, U.S. foreign policy, Osama bin Laden, will help young readers to understand the causes and consequences of the tragic events of 9/11. Includes color illustrations, a list containing "Countries that Lost Citizens in the World Trade Center Attacks," a glossary, additional resources on the subject, and an index. An excellent resource for school libraries. "This compact book does an excellent job of explaining the terrorist attacks on September 11th, but equally important is its presentation of the background that led to the events."—*Booklist*

420 *The Crisis of Islam: Holy War and Unholy Terror*
Lewis, Bernard.
Waterville, Maine: Thorndike Press, 2003. 232 pp.
Grades 11–12

Bernard Lewis, an internationally recognized Middle East historian, examines the historical roots of the resentments in the Islamic world that are often expressed by acts of terrorism. Of particular interest to readers would be the key events of the twentieth century leading up to violent confrontations, Israel's creation, the Cold War, the Iranian Revolution, the Soviet's defeat in Afghanistan, the Gulf War, and the September 11 attacks on the United States. Includes an index. Very informative.

421 *The Everlasting Hatred: The Roots of Jihad*
Lindsey, Hal.
Murrieta, California: Oracle House Publishing, 2002. 265 pp.
ISBN: 1931628157
Grades 9–12

The New York Times called Hal Lindsey the best-selling author in the world during the decade of the 1970s. From his Christian perspective, the author uses the Bible and historical data to recount the origin of Muslim hatred that goes back four thousand years. He contends that Islamic fundamentalism's purpose is to replace the Judeo-Christian world order with an Islamic world order. A relevant book for students interested in different points of view on this subject. Includes maps.

422 *Ground Zero*
Louis, Nancy.
Edina, Minnesota: Abdo Publishing Company, 2002. 48 pp.
ISBN: 1577656571
Grades 3–5

Part of the series titled "War on Terrorism," this book explains the September 11, 2001, terrorist attack on New York City, in which two airplanes were crashed into the World Trade Center. In addition, the aftermath of the attack, the search for and recovery of the victims, and plans for rebuilding the World Trade Center are also discussed. Includes color photographs, a glossary, an index, a list of related websites, and a very useful section on "Facts about the World Trade Center" and a "Timeline." Well organized and easy to understand. ". . . [W]ill help younger readers toward a basic understanding of what happened that day, not its causes."—*School Library Journal*

423 *September 11, 2001*
Santella, Andrew.
New York: Children's Press, 2002. 48 pp.
ISBN: 0516226924
Grades 4–6

The tragic events of September 11, 2001, when terrorists attacked the World Trade Center in New York City and the Pentagon outside Washington, are described step by step by the author in a dramatic way. The collapsing of the towers, reaction by President Bush, terrorism's history, Al Qaeda, world reaction, and war on terrorism are also discussed. Part of the series "Cornerstones of Freedom; Second Series," this book is an exceptional social studies resource for young readers. It will help young children learn about the 9/11 tragedy in a factual way. The "Timeline" listing events that took place on that day from 8:45 a.m. until 8:30 p.m. is a useful inclusion. Color illustrations, an index, a list of additional books and online sites, and a glossary, are included. Highly recommended for school libraries.

424 *Onward Muslim Soldiers: How Jihad Still Threatens America and the West*
Spencer, Robert.
Washington, D.C.: Regnery Publishing, Inc., 2003. 352 pp.
ISBN: 0895261006
Grades 11–12

Bestselling author Robert Spencer of *Islam Unveiled* describes in this book how Jihad warriors have established themselves in the United States as well as threatened Europe. The main theme of the book is that many Western analysts and policy makers refuse to see how dangerous the Islamic Jihad or sacred war is. A crucial subject of our time and a highly recommended book.

425 *America under Attack: September 11, 2001*
Stewart, Gail.
San Diego, California: Lucent Books, 2002. 96 pp.
ISBN: 1590182081
Grades 7–12

The author discusses the events of September 11, 2001, on the World Trade Center and the Pentagon, and the impact of these attacks on the American people. It also examines the history and personalities connected with terrorism in the United States and elsewhere in the world. The personal experiences of those involved, accounts from witnesses at the scene, from the American government and public, from political leaders and commentators abroad, are presented as well. Includes an annotated bibliography, notes, maps, black-and-white photographs, and an index. It is an excellent source for class discussion. Well researched and organized. Highly recommended.

426 *September 11, 2001: The Day that Changed America*
Wheeler, Jill C.
Edina, Minnesota: Abdo Publishers, 2002. 64 pp.
ISBN: 1577656563
Grades 4–7

The tragic events and immediate aftermath of the terrorist attacks on the World Trade Center towers in New York City, and the Pentagon near Washington, D.C., on September 11, 2001, are described in a very clear and simple manner. One of the chapters discusses "The Roots of Hatred." "Timeline of Terror, 9-11-01" lists all the events that took place pertaining to the terror attack from 8:45 a.m. to 8:30 p.m. on September 11. Includes a glossary, an index, and several dramatic color photographs. It is a very useful resource for young children who wish to get information regarding the tragic events that took place on 9/11. Highly recommended for school libraries.

427 *Islamic Fundamentalism*
Whitehood, Kim.

Broomall, Pennsylvania: Mason Crest Publishers, 2004. 120 pp.
Grades 10–12

An excellent overview of the emergence of the Islamic movement during the twentieth century. In contemporary Islam, fundamentalism represents one of the most important current trends. The differences between Islamists such as in Iran and moderates of Algeria, Indonesia, and Egypt are explained. It details the historical and political context that ignited the rise of modern fundamentalism. Color as well as black-and-white photographs contribute to the relevance of the text. A chronology and an index are included.

15

Women in Islam

Thirteen resources regarding the status and rights of Muslim women as defined by the Qur'an and Sunnah are provided in this chapter. Also included are resources that clarify some of the misconceptions that exist among some non-Muslims about Islamic women. Twelve of the resources are explicitly for the high school grade level. One is for the middle school grade level.

428 *The Islamic View of Women and the Family*
Abdul-Rauf, Muhammad.
New York: Robert Speller & Sons, 1979. 169 pp.
ISBN: 0831501561
Grades 11–12

The author was inspired to clarify the Islamic view of women after the United Nation's proclamation of the year 1975 as International Women's Year. As a result, Dr. Abudl-Rauf wrote this book, which is geared toward not only Muslims in the Americas, but for people of all faiths who are concerned with the moral breakdown in societies. This book definitely presents a Muslim man's position about Islamic women and their roles in today's societies and the necessity of maintaining high moral standings. Very interesting.

429 *The Position of Women in Islam: A Progressive View*
Ali, Syed Mohammed.
Albany, New York: State University of New York Press, 2004. 135 pp.
ISBN: 0791460959; ISBN (pbk.): 0791460967
Grades 11–12

According to the author of this book, the Qur'an and the Hadith, the two primary sources of Islamic law, place Muslim women on the same level as Muslim men. This is contrary to the general misconception that exists among some people. Women's rights in a variety of areas, including treatment by God; marriage; divorce; financial provisions; custody of children; participation in social, economic, legal and political activities, are discussed. This well-researched book presents the author's views with the objectivity required for this serious subject. Includes a list of useful references and an index.

430 *Tudung: Beyond Face Value*
Aliman, Salinah.
Singapore: Bridges Books, 2002. 94 pp.
ISBN: 9810463952
Grades 7–12
Forty-two Muslims and non-Muslims express their views regarding the mystery of the headscarf worn by Muslim women, called the *tudung*. Their personal experiences with the tudung and the struggle to combat stereotypes are also discussed. Beautifully illustrated with color photographs, it is a fascinating must-read book for those who wish to explore the factors behind the practice of wearing tudung. Highly recommended. "A beautiful book, one of those 'must reads.'"—Linda Delgado, president, Islamic Writers Alliance.

431 *Woman in the Shade of Islam*
Al-Sheha, Abdul Rahman; rendered into English by Mohammed Said Dabas.
Shamis Mushait, Saudi Arabia: Islamic Educational Center, 2002. 120 pp.
ISBN: 9960800237
Grades 11–12
Motivated high school students as well as adults will appreciate the organization and perspective of this book that presents the Islamic views about women, and to what extent women are respected and protected in Islam. The reader can easily find a topic by scanning the topical headings without reading page by page even though the book does not have a table of contents. The major issues discussed are: woman's equality with men, historical status of women throughout the ages, misconceptions about women in Islam, and women's rights in Islam. An excellent resource.

432 *Gender Equity in Islam: Basic Principles*
Badawi, Jamal A.

[USA]: Soltan, 2004. 70 pp.
ISBN: 0892591595
Grades 9–12

An overview of the status and rights of Muslim women as defined by the Qur'an and Sunnah, are presented by the author. In addition to summarizing the role of women in Muslim society, Dr. Badawi discusses the spiritual, social, economic, and political aspects of women's position in Islam. The role of Islamic scholars in their approach to women's issues is also explained. Includes a very useful bibliography for additional information on the subject of gender equity in Islam.

433 *Inside the Kingdom: My Life in Saudi Arabia*
bin Ladin, Carmen.
New York: Warner books, 2004. 206 pp.
ISBN: 0446577081
Grades 9–12

Exceptionally written, this is a wonderful story of Carmen bin Ladin, who was married to one of Osama bin Laden's half brothers. Since she was of Swiss and Iranian descent, she was always considered to be a foreigner in the Bin Laden clan. Clearly written, unadulterated account of the life of a woman living in Saudi Arabia is portrayed in this book. The subservient role of women is also discussed. Will appeal particularly to female readers. Includes family photographs in black and white. "This intimate memoir of one woman's spiritual reawakening and odyssey has best seller written all over it." — *Booklist*

434 *Nine Parts of Desire: The Hidden World of Islamic Women*
Brooks, Geraldine.
New York: Anchor Books, 1996. 255 pp.
ISBN: 0385475772
Grades 11–12

A prizewinning foreign correspondent for *The Wall Street Journal*, Geraldine Brooks spent six years covering the Middle East through wars, and other news events. During her stay she got very interested in learning about the daily lives of Muslim women. In this captivating book, she relates her journey and observations regarding the women behind the veils, and the contradictory religious, social, political, and cultural forces that shape their lives. The book illustrates how Islam's holiest text, the Qur'an, has been misinterpreted and misused by some Muslim males to justify repression of women in Islam. Includes a glossary of terms, a select bibliography, and an index. "A wonderful writer and thinker; the observations she makes and conclusions she reaches open both our eyes and minds to understanding Muslim women anew."—*Booklist*

435 *Women Claim Islam: Creating Islamic Feminism through Literature*
Cooke, Miriam.
New York: Routledge, 2001. 175 pp.
ISBN: 0415925533; ISBN (pbk.): 0415925541
Grades 11–12
The stories and autobiographies of contemporary Muslim women are presented in a way to create discussion and debate. Each chapter has a conclusion to help the reader. The six chapters contain information about how Muslim women have begun to critique Islamic beliefs and establish their own individuality. Very scholarly and recommended for advanced readers only. Includes an index.

436 *The Honor of Women in Islam*
da Costa, Yusuf.
Washington, D.C.: Islamic Supreme Council of America, 2002. 90 pp.
ISBN: 1930409060
Grades 11–12
This book is truly enlightening for those who wish to obtain an informative understanding of the respect and love for women inherent in the Islamic faith. Includes a glossary of terms, bibliography, a general index, and an index of verses from Qur'an and Hadith.

437 *The Rights of Women in Islam*
Engineer, Asghar Ali.
New York: New Dawn Press, 2004. 232 pp.
ISBN: 1932705015
Grades 11–12
In the Islamic religion, women's rights are discussed in detail both in the Qur'an and in the formulations of Islamic law. The Qur'an awards equal status to both sexes. However, according to the author, "the theologians ignored the context and made men superior in the absolute sense." The author believes in the need of interpreting the text from the Qur'an correctly. In this revised edition, he explains and critically evaluates Muslim women's rights pertaining to marriage, inheritance, divorce, custody of children, property, and much more. In addition, the author recaptures the original

spirit of the Qur'anic laws with regard to the male-female relationship. Includes an interesting appendix that discusses the law of marriage and divorce among Muslims, Christians, and Parsis in India. An index is included. Well-researched. ". . . [R]efutes Islamic fundamentalist views that men are superior to women." — *Booklist*

438 *Price of Honor: Muslim Women Lift the Veil of Silence on the Islamic World*
Goodwin, Jan.
New York: Plume, 2003. 351 pp.
ISBN: 0452283779
Grades 11–12
This extraordinary book is written by an award-winning journalist, Jan Goodwin, who traveled through ten Islamic countries and interviewed hundreds of Muslim women from many walks of life, including professionals, peasants, royalty, and rebels. She shares in this book the findings from her interviews regarding the treatment of women. These interviews are both fascinating and disturbing. The book includes a map and an index. "Findings are profoundly disturbing and center on the enormous influence of radical Islam." — *Booklist*

439 *The Muslim Woman's Handbook*
Khattab, Huda.
London: Ta-Ha, 1994. 70 pp.
ISBN: 1897940009
Grades 10–12
Written by a British Muslim writer, this well-organized book is a practical guide to daily life as a Muslim woman. Topics such as purity and cleanliness, Hijab, social life, education and work, marriage and divorce, and health are explained. This book is aimed at born-Muslims and converts alike. It clarifies some of the misconceptions by non-Muslims. Each chapter is followed by a short summary. A bibliography, an index, and a glossary are included.

440 *The Trouble with Islam: A Muslim's Call for Reform in Her Faith*
Manji, Irshad.
New York: St. Martin's Press, 2003. 229 pp.
ISBN: 0312326998
Grades 9–12

Fundamental, devout Muslims would not consider this author a Muslim since she is a lesbian, in spite of the fact that she is a well-known journalist, television personality, and a writer-in-residence at the University of Toronto. It is a thought-provoking book that explores problems with those who practice Islam and suggests remedies for these problems. "Her sassy but earnest perspective seems a godsend." —*Booklist*. "Her book will be an unsettling read for most of her fellow Muslims." —*Publishers Weekly*

16

Internet Resources

The following list of ninety-seven websites is arranged alphabetically by chapters.

ART, ARCHITECTURE, AND SCIENCE

441 The National Museum: Riyadh, Saudi Arabia
www.Saudimuseum.com
The site offers a vast picture gallery of exhibition hall displays such as Islam and the Arabian Peninsula, The First and Second Saudi State, and Muhammad's Museum. Virtual tours are available for each of the Exhibition Halls cited. For example: the channel, Selected Pieces from Our Collection, displays pots, jewelry, and artifacts. In addition, there are pages of publications sold in the Museum Shop, pictures of historical and archeological ruins, architecture and much more. The site is very impressive and offers a wealth of information and visual imagery.

442 Islamic Arts and Architecture (IAAO)
www.islamicart.com
This is a marvelous site with extensive audio and videos, articles, and historical data. The website is designed to provide information on arts and architecture. It also has a strong commitment to research and service. A non-profit organization dedicated to providing information on arts and architecture, this site offers short films that can be downloaded, and it covers many areas of Islam and related topics such as the Five Pillars of Islam and

Islamic faith, customs, and culture, misconceptions and myths about Islam, and Jihad. This is a very interesting and informative website. It is appropriate for Muslims and non-Muslims.

BIOGRAPHY

443 Following Muhammed
www.unc.edu/~cernst/islam.htm
This site is maintained by Carl W. Ernst, a distinguished professor of Religious Studies at the University of North Carolina. He is the author of *Following Muhammad: Rethinking Islam in the Contemporary World* as well as other publications about Islam. The web page offers links to the Internet site that he used when writing *Following Muhammad*. It also contains a broader range of online sources on Islam such as Internet Resources for the Study of Islam and Resources for Islamic Studies and much more. It is an invaluable website.

444 Prophet Muhammad
www.muhammad.net
This is an educational website regarding the biography, mission and message of the Prophet Muhammad. It contains introductory articles, biographies of Muhammed, 500 *Ahadith*, archives and much more. It provides extensive resources for research regarding the Prophet Muhammad.

CURRICULAR RESOURCES

445 Arab World and Islamic Resources and School Services (AWAIR)
www.dnaI.com~gui/awairproductinf
This marvelous site is for educators of the elementary to pre-college level. It is a reliable site for teaching materials. AWAIR also publishes several books and videos about the Middle East and Islam.

446 Council on Islamic Education (CIE)
www.cie.org
CIE is a resource organization for K–12 educators, textbook publishers, education officials and policy makers, curriculum developers, and other educational professionals. There are a number of invaluable resources to help teach about Islam, Muslim history, and related topics.

This is one of the most beneficial websites for materials needed by professional educators.

447 Islam: Empire of Faith
www.pbs.org/empires/islam
Islam: Empire of Faith is an extremely useful site that would appeal to junior and senior high school students. It is an online companion to the PBS film, *Empire of Faith*, that is about the faith, culture, innovations, and the people of Islam.

448 Knowing Islam through Muslims: Islamic Learning Media 2005
www.IslamicLearningMedia.com
Grades 8–12
Book categories on this website are: Foundations of Islamic faith; Life hereafter; Pillars of Islam; Qur'an & sunnah; Islamic history; Islamic world; Muslim family; Islam & science; Reference; Biographies; Contemporary issues.

449 Middle East Policy Council
www.mepc.org
An important and valuable site, Middle East Policy Council was founded in 1981 to promote and expand public discussion and provide academic issues about the United States concerning issues affecting U.S. policy in the Middle East. It is an excellent resource for secondary school educators for information on how to teach students about the Arab world and the religion of Islam.

450 Purdue Extension: Terrorism and Children
www.ces.purdue.edu/terrorism
The Purdue University Extension: Knowledge to Go focuses on aspects of terrorism and how to help children cope with the stress and threats terrorism presents. It also offers parents and teachers strategies that can be used in regard to terrorism. Multimedia (audio and video) and articles make this an invaluable resource on this topic.

451 The Islamic Garden
www.islamicgarden.com/page1002.html
This site specifically provides educational links for a Muslim children. It can be translated into prominent world languages. There are downloads for Muslim children, and about twenty-two different channels present a variety of stories, games and activities. This is a remarkable site for educators and parents.

452 Yemen Webdate: Yemen Fiction
www.aiys.org/webdate/fiction.html
    This is an excellent resource about Yemen fiction. The fiction is written
by Yemeni and non-Yemeni authors about aspects of Yemeni society. A
reader will find story adaptations, a Yemen Webdate Archive Link, and
much more.

FICTION AND FOLKLORE

453 Al-Janna The Garden: A Muslim Vision of Paradise
www.siskiyous.edu/class/
    Islamic paradise, Al-Janna, can be found on this web page. Pictures are
available for additional information such as: a study of Afterlife Folklore in
Judaism, Christianity, and Islam. It is a fascinating and unique website with
a quiz on the information at the end.

GENERAL REFERENCE

454 About Islam
http://islam.about.com/od/ramadan/
    One of the topical channels provides a wealth of articles and links to Is-
lam and Islamic festivals. This is an essential resource for information
about Islam.

455 Aljazeera.net English
http://English.aljazeera.net
    Often controversial, but very prominent in the networks worldwide. Al-
jazeera often reports news not found on any of the other websites. The target audience is aimed at the mainstream population of the world. It offers
current news on world affairs, views of the news, scientific developments,
economy, culture, and weather.

456 AMIDEAST
www.amideast.org
    Headquartered in Washington, D.C., America-Mideast Educational and
Training Services, Inc., is a private, nonprofit organization designed to promote mutual understanding and cooperation between America and Islamic
countries. The primary countries are those in the Middle East and North

Africa. AMIDEAST provides educational opportunities for cultural exchange between Arabs and North Americans. It also publishes a number of books for all age groups.

457 Arabia.com
www.arabia.com/index.cgi/english.html

This site is owned by Arabia Online. Its target audience is the Arab world and the broader international community interested in the Arab world. It can be read in English and Arabic. The website covers a wide range of topics with continuous news, sports, and business coverage, in-depth and entertaining lifestyle reports, books, music and movie information. In addition, it has reference channels such as Arab world country information, an Islam channel, special topics, events, TV guide, weather, e-cards, and even horoscopes. It contains a wealth of useful information.

458 Arabji.com
www.arabji.com/

It contains a Pan Arab Directory on a multitude of information about the Arab world such as business, economy, government and politics, entertainment and sports, society and culture. There is also an Arab Countries Directory covering twenty-two countries.

459 Astrolabe.com
www.astrolabe.com

This site is a directory and e-store. It is a complete online resource for Islamic books, audio tapes, videos, and products of interest about the Islamic religion.

460 BBC News World Edition
http://news.bbc.co.uk

BBC News is a renowned source that not only offers extensive coverage of international news, but also reports on Islamic fundamentalist activities. This is an excellent resource for up-to-date information about the Middle East.

461 Center for Middle Eastern Studies
http://menic.utexas.edu/menic/cmes

The center was established by the U.S. Department of Education to promote a better understanding of the Middle East. The University of Texas at Austin has developed this notable site. It provides information for its

Multilanguage Studies program for Arabic, Hebrew, Persian, and Turkish studies. Graduate and undergraduate program information concerning these studies is available. In addition, it provides research and instructional materials.

462 CNN.com

www.cnn.com

This site focuses on news and is usually the source of breaking news about terrorism and other world events. A searchable archive of past articles is also available that makes it an ideal resource for researchers.

463 Encyclopedia of the Orient

http://i-cias.com/e.o/saudi.htm

The Encyclopedia of the Orient features resources about Saudi Arabia. It contains a wealth of information: articles on the political situation, economy, health and education, religions and peoples, geography, and history.

464 International Institute of Islamic Thought

www.iiit.org

This site is available in English, Arabic, and French. It was developed primarily for people in higher education. The website contains news, media, upcoming events for Muslims, new books about Islam, etc.

465 Introduction to the Arab World

www.middleastnews.com/introarab101.html or www.MiddleEastNews.com

Sponsored by The Arab American Guide.com and maintained by Middle East News, this site is an excellent comprehensive introduction to all aspects of the Arab World. Information can be found on geography, history, Islam, education, literature, the sciences, mathematics, astronomy, and much more.

466 Islam 101

www.islam101.com

It is an invaluable educational site about Islam that depicts the way of people's lives, their civilization, and culture. Features include Views.Com, downloads, theology, human relations, comparative religion, and much more.

467 Islam For Today.com

www.islamfortoday.com

The object of this site is to promote the theology of Islam to Westerners seeking knowledge and understanding of the religion. The information contains a guide to the religion of Islam, Muslim history and civilizations, the rights of women in Islam, Islam in the West and around the world today. In addition, there is information about Muslim schools and family life.

468 Islam online.net

www.islamonline.net/english/index.shtml

The mission of this web page is to create a unique, global Islamic site that provides services to Muslims and non-Muslims in several languages. The site contains references for everything that deals with Islam, its sciences, civilization and nation. It is a very comprehensive source.

469 Islam, Islamic Studies, Arab, and Religion

www.arches.uga.edu/~godlas/islamwest.html

Professor Alan Godlas, University of Georgia, maintains this site, Islam, The Modern World, and the West: Contemporary Topics. The table of contents lists a wide variety of topics—General Considerations; Islam, Peace, Jihad, Violence and Terrorism; Islam and Democracy; Islam and Human Rights; Islam, Exclusivism, and Pluralism; Islam and Women; Islam and Slavery; Islam and Ecology and more. It is quite comprehensive and includes essays and links to various topics.

470 Islamic Learning Media 2005: Knowing Islam through Muslims: The Library Project.

www.IslamicLearning Media.com

Started in Kentucky in 2002, Islamic Learning Media provides an avenue for Muslim authors to publish and distribute their books. These authors are respected Islamic scholars who bring significant expertise and experience to this Library Project, which is divided into eleven series covering various aspects of Islam. The titles are: Foundations of Islamic Faith, Life Hereafter, Pillars of Islam, Qur'an & Sunnah, Islamic History, Islamic World, Muslim Family, Islam & Science, Reference, Biographies, Contemporary Issues. These will be very helpful for readers ages thirteen and up.

471 Islamtoday.com

www.islamtoday.com/

A wealth of information about Islam can be found on this site. It has explanations about Islamic beliefs.

472 Middle East Research and Information Project (MERIP)
www.merip.org
MERIP attempts to promote an understanding of the Middle East and
eliminate stereotypes and misconceptions about the area. By soliciting writings and views from authors from the Middle East, a wide range of social,
political, and cultural issues are addressed.

473 Minnesota Public Radio
http://new.minnesota.publicradio.org/features/2004/04/09_williamsb_
    conference/
MPR News focuses on topics of interest for specific groups. At the time
of this writing, the focus was on Islam: a way of life; but the information
concerning Islam constantly changes due to current events. The site usually
offers information about Islamic events or personalities.

474 Palestinian Academic Study of International Affairs (PASSIA)
www.passia.org/
The Palestinian Academic Society for the Study of International Affairs
is an Arab non-profit institution that was founded in 1987 by a group of
Palestinian academics and intellectuals in Jerusalem. The web page contains information on Palestinian facts and figures, history, a historical timeline, personalities, maps and a photography archive.

475 Palestinian National Authority (PNA)
www.pna.gov.ps/index.asp
PNA is the official homepage of the Palestinian National Authority. It
claims to offer current news relevant to the Palestinians and reports gener-
ated by the PNA.

476 Rizwi's Bibliography for Medieval Islam
http://us.geocities.com/rfaizer/biblio/
Maintained by Rizwi S. Fraizer, Ph.D, (McGill), one can find a well-
organized, extensive bibliography of resources for reference such as significant books and articles related to Medieval Islam. The categories of the
resources are Introduction, Islamic History, Islamic Thought, and Islamic
Institutions.

477 Talk Islam
http://talkislam.com

This is an invaluable site because it is a library of Islam-related and general websites and links on the Internet categorized by topic and subject matter. This excellent website can be used to find information on the Islamic religion, organizations, mosques, articles on the Islamic world, new books and DVDs on Islam, comparative religion studies, and much more.

478 The Arab World: Your Web Guide to Everything Arab
http://cecilmarie.web.prw.net/arabworld/
This site is an excellent introductory source about the Arab world with a vast collection of varied categories. The topics are Arts and Humanities, Arabic Language, Islamic History, Arab and Middle Eastern Recipes. The Web Resources link offers a huge collection of sites about Arab history, culture, news, education, travel, and more. It is truly an essential resource about the Arab world.

479 The Middle East Research Institute (MEMRI)
http://memri.org
This is another multi-lingual site enriched with information about the Middle East. MEMRI is an independent, non-partisan, non-profit organization, it explores the Middle East through the regions' media, and bridges the language barriers of all the trends in the region. There are videos, cartoons, specific reports on Middle Eastern countries, the latest topics concerning the Middle East, and more. It is an outstanding resource of information for everyone.

480 The University of Delaware Library: Islam: A Research Guide
www2.lib.udel.edu/subj/phil/resguide/islam.htm
This website is maintained by the reference department of the University of Delaware. It offers topical channels about Islam such as Starting Point for Research, Country Information, Law, Koran, and United States professional organizations. This is a truly useful link for research.

481 The World Factbook
www.cia.gov/cia/publications/factbook
Maintained by the Central Intelligence Agency of the United States, The World Factbook provides basic information on the countries of the world. By using a pull-down tab, one can research a specific country's information such as background, geography, people, economics, government, and maps. It is an excellent resource for research about specific Islamic countries.

482 United Association for Studies and Research (UASR)
www.uasr.org
    The United Association for Studies and Research, Inc., was created in
1989 by a number of scholars, journalists, and businessmen for the study of
on-going issues in the Middle East. It is a non-profit organization that examines the causes of conflict in the Middle East and Africa as well as the
political trends that mold the area's future, and the relationship of the region to other nations. A wide range of topics can be researched: Muslims in
the United States, Islam and the West, interviews, policy papers, and more.

GEOGRAPHY

483 About.com
http://geography.about.com/library/weekly/220398.Ltm
    About.com is a directory that offers hundreds of subject topics. This link
offers information pertaining to Islamic Geography in the Middle Ages.
There are link sites to other sources as well.

484 Arab.net
www.arab.net/lebanon
    This is a valuable resource on the geography of Lebanon. In addition,
there are links to history, business, culture, government, and much more.

485 Statistical, Economic and Social Research and Training Centre for Is-
      lamic Countries (SESRTCIC)
http://sesrtcic.org
    It provides general information about the geography, economy, and de-
mography about Syria. In addition, there are many other informative links.

486 Syria Today
www.syriatoday.com/home.htm
    Syria Today is a very comprehensive site for one interested in current
and past information about Syria. In addition, it has links in regard to government, geography, history, and tourism.

487 Yemen Embassy.org
www.yemenembassy.org
    The Embassy of Yemen maintains this homepage to provide information
on the country, the people, culture, government, economy, and Yemeni-U.S.

relationships. The channels fall under the following headings: Welcome, Explore the Embassy, Issues of Interest, Links and Resources, and much more about the country of Yemen.

488 Arab Countries: U.A.E.
www.hejleh.com/countries/uae.html
Country and People of United Arab Emirates offers a wealth of information about the people and their country, their business and economy, human rights and politics, education, tourism, and governmental organization. In addition, there are links to other sites. It is an invaluable resource about the geography of U.A.E.

489 Lonely Planet: Arab countries
http://search.lonelyplanet.com/query.html?col=full&ht
This website contains a directory for Arab and other countries with on-line guides for each country. This is an essential resource for geographical information about Arab countries.

490 The Hashemite Kingdom of Jordan Department of Statistics (DOS)
www.dos.gov.jo
The site is dedicated to statistical information about Jordan. It also contains a brief history, publications, and press releases.

HISTORY

491 American Muslim Alliance (AMA)
www.amaweb.org
A site strictly for Muslims, it is to promote political involvement in all aspects of North American politics. The object is to make Muslims become aware and active in U.S. politics.

492 American Muslims Intent on Learning and Activism (AMILA)
www.icna.com/
This website provides information on current events of interest to Muslims, profiles of famous North American Muslims such as Malcolm X, and political concerns of Muslims. It also contains information about outreach programs for Muslims who were incarcerated in North American prisons.

493 American-Arab Anti Discrimination Committee (ADC)
www.adc.org
    An outstanding site for people of all backgrounds, faiths, and ethnicities
can be found on this website. It is committed to empowering Arab Americans and defending the civil rights of all people of Arab heritage in the
United States. The organization fights anti-American stereotyping in the
media and actions of hate.

494 Arab-Islamic History
www.al-bab.com/arab/history.htm
    A comprehensive collection of data links on Arab-Islamic history can
be found on this website. Examples of topics covered are the Pre-Islamic
Period, the Birth of Islam, Islamic Expansion, the Early Caliphate,
Umayyad and Abbasids, Islam in Europe, the Crusades, Fatimads and
Mamluks, Turks and Ottomans, and Aspects of Imperialism.

495 Internet Islam History Sourcebook
www.fordham.edu/halsall/islam/islamsbook.html
    It provides a subset of texts derived from three other on-line source-
books: Internet Ancient History Sourcebook, Internet Medieval Sourcebook plus Islam History Section, and Internet Modern History Sourcebook.
For students needing help, there are links to Ancient History, Medieval
Studies, and Modern History. It is a very detailed, comprehensive resource.

INTERRELIGIOUS STUDIES

496 Beliefnet.com
http://beliefnet.com
    Beliefnet.com is an independent, multi-faith e-community and is not af-
filiated with a particular religion or spiritual movement. Information about
the leading religions of the world, religions' tools, religious comparisons,
and a wealth of other information can be explored by using this site. It is a
wonderful resource for inter-religious exploration.

497 Crescent Project
www.arabim.org/links.cfm
    This site was founded in 1993 by a Lebanese pastor to equip Christians
to reach out to the Muslim community. It was originally known as Arab In-

ternational Ministry. The site contains a multitude of links such as: Information about Islam, Training and Educating, Islamic Websites for Qur'an and Hadith, and much more.

498 Discover Islam
www.beconvinced.com

This is a useful site for non-Muslims to become informed about the religion of Islam. It discusses the relationship between Christianity and Islam, the beliefs of Islam as well as the top misconceptions. It is a useful website for inter-religious comparisons.

499 Islam America
www.islamamerica.org

Maintained by Dar Al Islam, a non-profit organization, the purpose of this site is to promote understanding between Muslims and non-Muslims in The United States. It includes recent articles on Islam in America, politics, culture, perspectives, Islamic science, and history.

500 Muslim America Society
www.masnet.org

This is an excellent website that presents a wide range of topics from current news to the practice of Islam. The purpose of this site is to present the message of Islam to Muslims and non-Muslims and promote understanding between them.

501 The Bible and the Qur'an: An Historical Comparison
http://debate.org.uk/topics/history/bib-qur/contents.htm

This is a site owned by the Hyde Park Christian researchers in the United Kingdom. The primary function of the website is to provide academic study of all issues relevant to Islam and Christianity. It offers resources in regard to debatable topics about the Bible and the Qur'an. This information is exhaustive with links to UK Islamic sites, links to Christian resources, debate topics and articles, and much more.

502 The Good Way
www.the-good-way.com/eng/article/a13.htm

The purpose of this site is to present a comparative study of the Christian and Muslim attitudes toward Jesus Christ. It also asks questions: "Do you know the best way to God? Is it the way of the Torah, the way of the Gospel or the way of the Qur'an?" Many links to books and articles are provided to address the cited questions.

ISLAMIC FAITH AND PRACTICE

503 A Brief Illustrated Guide to Understanding Islam
www.islam-guide.com
This site has been specifically designed for non-Muslims who would like to understand Islam, Muslims, and the Holy Qur'an. It contains the chapter of the book that has the same title as the website. The book contains comprehensive information regarding Islam, references, bibliography, and illustrations. The information can also be read on the Internet in other languages. It is a very informative website.

504 About Islam
http://islam.about.com
About Islam offers an Internet guide to Islam, which covers feature articles, website guides, and discussion forums. Some of the interesting topics covered in this website are art, history, law, Muhammad, and the Qur'an.

505 Al-Islam
http://al-islam.org
This is a useful site for both Muslims and non-Muslims. It provides non-Muslims an introduction to Islam, and advanced knowledge about Islam to Muslims.

506 Canadian Islamic Congress (CIC)
www.cicnow.com
Established by The Canadian Islamic Congress, this site promotes, coordinates, facilitates, demonstrates, and implements the teaching and practices of Islam.

507 Discover Islam
www.sultan.org
A wealth of up-to-date information regarding Islam can be found on this site. The lists of topics are innumerable. There are site links to some famous Islamic scholars, audios, and much more.

508 Frontline PBS: Muslims

www.pbs.org/wgbh/pages/frontline/shows/muslims

PBS provides an essential resource on the Internet that examines Islam's worldwide resurgence through stories of diverse Muslims struggling to define the role of Islam in their lives and societies. It examines contemporary Islam by an introduction; major themes such as Islam and the West, Islamic belief and practice, women and Islam; profiles and interviews with Muslims, and frequently asked questions. The site is very informative.

509 IslamiCity

www.islamicity.com

It is a great reference site for information about Islam that lists extensive videos, audio narratives, articles, etc. A wealth of information for Muslims as well as non-Muslims is provided. One must become a member to view the videos.

510 Islamic Assembly of North America (IANA)

www.iananet.org

Established in 1993 by a number of individuals who were concerned and active in the field of *dawah*, propagating Islam, in the United States and Canada, this site provides news, activities of the members, and publications of IANA. Although the site has been designed for Muslims, the publications might be of interest to non-Muslims.

511 Islamic Food and Nutrition Council of America (IFANCA)

www.ifanca.org

An invaluable site, it provides support to Muslims and their communities. It is an association of Muslim organizations and individuals to develop social and outreach programs for Muslims living in the United States. It would be of more interest to Muslims than non-Muslims.

512 Islamic Foundation of America (IFA)

www.sunnah.org/about/Default.htm

Founded by a group of concerned Muslims from many backgrounds and specialties, IFA is striving to promote the unity of Muslims and understanding and awareness through education. The site offers a variety of topical links from cartoons to prayer resources, e-cards to shopping, and more. It is a very diverse and interesting URL.

513 Islamic Server of MSA-USC
www.usc.edu/dept/MSA

The Muslim Students Association at USC maintains this site. It is primarily an extensive collection of information about all aspects of Islam. Basic topics include: The Fundamentals of Islam, Special Topics about Islam, Comparative Analysis of Religion, The Muslims. It is very well organized for research and scholarly endeavors.

514 Islamic World
http://islamic-world.net

The official website of Khalifah Institute, an organization whose members are dedicated to practice and promote Islam, was created in 2000. The site has over 3,000 web pages, making it the world's largest Islamic website. There are approximately 33,000 links to other Islamic websites. This is an excellent resource on topics too numerous to describe.

515 Latino American Dawah Organization (LADO)
www.latinodawah.org

It is a wonderful site founded in 1997 for converts to Islam. It provides information about the legacy of Islam in Spain and Latin America as well as information about Islam.

516 Profile of Saudi Arabia: Islam
www.saudiembassy.org.uk/profile-of-saudia-arabia/islam/introduction.htm

This site was created by the Royal Embassy of Saudi Arabia in London to develop an appreciation of Islamic history and culture. It is an excellent source containing topics such as: Introduction, The Coming of the Prophet, The Rise of Islam, the Community of the Faithful, The Five Pillars of Islam, Saudi Arabia: Islam's Heartland, Guardian of the Holy Places, and Understanding Islam and the Muslims. It is written in an easily understandable manner.

517 The Islam Page
www.islamworld.net

This is a very interesting site for non-Muslims as well as Muslims. A broad range of topical headings from the Holy Qur'an to Advice on Studying Islam Abroad is given.

518 The Sunnah Islamic Page
www.al-sunnah.com

The Sunnah Islamic Page is for non-Muslims as well as followers of the faith. It is also available in other languages. It contains an eclectic source of information about Islam and terrorism on audio cassettes and in books.

MUSLIMS IN THE WEST

519 Council on American-Islamic Relations (CAIR)
www.cair-net.org

An essential resource on the Internet for American Muslims, this site also presents an Islamic perspective on issues of importance to the American public. The mission of this site is to enhance the understanding of Islam, promote dialogue, protect civil liberties, empower American Muslims and promote justice and mutual understanding. It was established to promote an accurate image of Muslims as well as the religion of Islam. It is primarily for Muslims.

520 International Information Programs (USINFO.STATE.GOV)
http://usinfo.state.gov/products/pubs/muslimlife/homepage.htm

This is a wonderful website for research for Muslims and non-Muslims about Muslims in the United States. The information ranges from family life, Muslim communities, education, varieties of worship, the world of work, or even into the mainstream of North American life.

521 Islamic Circle of North America (ICNA)
www.icna.org

Established in 1971, this site provides encouragement and personal development to follow the Islamic system of life as spelled out in the Qur'an and the Sunnah of the Prophet Muhammad. It is a valuable site for Muslims living in Western countries.

522 Islamic Society of North American (ISNA)
www.isna.net

This site is primarily for Muslims to become a part of an association of Muslim organizations to unify a platform for presenting Islam; supporting Muslim communities; developing educational, social and outreach programs; and fostering good relations with other religious communities and civic and service organizations.

523 Muslim Public Affairs Council (MPAC)

www.mpac.org

This site offers resources about the establishment of a vibrant American Muslim community that can enrich the American society through promoting Islamic values. At the same time, it provides information to educate the North American public.

524 Terrorism: Questions and Answers

http://cfrterrorism.org/home

Operated by The Markle Foundation and The Council on Foreign Relations, this is a non-profit group that studies communications and media. One can find a wealth of information about different terrorist organizations and their activities throughout the world. There are also question-and-answer sheets providing information on specific terrorist groups. This is a user-friendly website.

525 View Islam.com

www.viewislam.com

Voluminous information about different aspects of Islam on several very comprehensive Islamic websites can be found on this web page. It is a good resource for English speaking non-Muslims and newly converted English-speaking Muslims from Western countries.

NATION OF ISLAM

526 Nation of Islam

www.noi.org

This is the official site for the Nation of Islam. It includes a brief history, official Nation of Islam articles from the Reverend Louis Farrakhan, study guides, and contact information for Nation of Islam mosques.

QUR'AN

527 Quran.org

www.quran.org

For people interested in information about the Qur'an, this is an ideal site. It includes links to resources on the Qur'an, online translations, browsers, and commentary.

528 The Koran
www.hti.umich.edu/k/koran
   This site is specifically devoted to an electronic version of the Holy Qur'an, translated by M. H. Shakir and published by Tahrike Tarsile Qur'an Inc., in 1983. There are four main links for research: simple searches for single words or phrases, proximity searches for co-occurrences of two or three words or phrases, boolean searches for combinations of two or three words, and browse the Qur'an.

529 Understanding Islam
http://understanding-islam.com
   In addition to presenting the explanation of Islam in the light of the Qur'an and the Sunnah of the Prophet, this site posts discussions, articles, links to other sites and a translation of the Qur'an.

RESISTANCE VERSUS TERRORISM

530 Central Intelligence Agency (CIA): The War on Terrorism
www.cia.gov/terrorism
   Maintained by the CIA, this site offers official CIA statements and information on CBRN (chemical, biological, radiological, or nuclear attacks) and biological warfare. Some additional links are: Terrorism FAQs, a Chemical, Biological/Radiological Incident Handbook and related links concerning terrorism.

531 Intelligence Resource Program (FAS)
www.fas.org/irp/threat/terror.htm
   This is a link to the Federation of American Scientists concerning terrorism — the background and threat assessments. An extensive amount of information can be found such as: General Information, September 11 and the Aftermath, Middle East Terror, Chemical and Biological Weapons, Related Resources and more. It is a very user-friendly website.

533 U.S. Department of State: Counterterrorism Office
www.state.gov/s/ct
   This website focuses on the U.S. policy dealing with terrorism and the kidnapping of American citizens. Other topic headings include information on: Counterterrorism Current Events, the Global Coalition Against Terrorism, an Operation Directorate, the Counterterrorism Finance and Designation Unit,

Homeland Security, Countering Terrorism, and Related Sites. Of significance is a current list of foreign terrorist organizations.

533 University of Michigan Documents Center: America's War Against Terrorism
www.lib.umich.edu/govdocs/usterror.html
Maintained by the University of Michigan Library, this site offers a multitude of articles and links with regard to terrorism. The topics begin with information on the September 11th attacks and topical information since then. It is very diverse and comprehensive.

WOMEN IN ISLAM

534 Arab Women Connect (AWC)
www.arabwomenconnect.org
This Arabic/English website contains studies, reports, and statistics on Arab women. The site offers the latest news about Arab women, activists, and Arab women in government. It is a very detailed site viewing the roles of modern Arab women.

535 Femininity Muslim Style: Women in Islam
www.geocities.com/TheTropics/Resort/2389
Featured on this website are pictures of traditional women's costumes in Muslim countries. The pictures can be downloaded for presentation or used to give a researcher knowledge about traditional Muslim women's clothes in various Islamic countries around the world.

536 Muslims Women's League (MWL)
www.mwlusa.org
An extremely useful site that has been created for Muslim women. It has been designed to help women implement the values of Islam and reclaim the status of women as free, equal, and vital contributors to society.

Author Index

The numbers refer to entries, not pages

Geographic Index

The numbers refer to entries, not pages

Grade Index

The numbers refer to entries, not pages

Illustrator and Photographer Index

The numbers refer to entries, not pages

Subject Index

The numbers refer to entries, not pages

Title Index

The numbers refer to entries, not pages

About the Authors

Rajinder Garcha, born and raised in Tanzania, received her associate degree from Highridge Teachers' Training College in Nairobi, Kenya, and taught elementary school for six years in Dar es Salaam, Tanzania. She received her BS degree in educational studies and her MLS in library and information science from Kent State University in Ohio. She worked at Kent State University libraries for several years prior to becoming a faculty member of the University of Toledo. From 2001 to 2002, she was the interim dean of university libraries at the University of Toledo and has had numerous articles published in refereed journals. She has a married daughter, a son, and two grandsons and resides in Toledo, Ohio.

Patricia Yates Russell is the senior ESL specialist of the American Language Institute at the University of Toledo and was the first teacher hired for the program in 1977. She has held elementary and secondary teacher certification for the states of Illinois, West Virginia, and Ohio.